COMBAT ARMS

MODERN

FIGHTERS

Edited by RAY BONDS

Prentice Hall Press
New York   London   Toronto   Sydney   Tokyo

A Salamander Book

Prentice Hall Press
Gulf + Western Building
One Gulf + Western Plaza
New York, NY 10023

An Arco Military Book
Published by the Prentice Hall Trade Division.

PRENTICE HALL PRESS and colophon are registered
trademarks of Simon & Schuster Inc.

Originally published in 1988 in the United Kingdom by
Salamander Books Ltd., 52 Bedford Row, London WC1R 4LR.

This book may not be sold outside the United States
of America or Canada.

Library of Congress Cataloging in Publication Data

Modern fighters.
    (Combat arms) (An Arco military book)
    1. Fighter planes. 2. Jet planes, Military.
    1. Bonds, Ray. II. Series. III. Series.
Arco military book.
UG1242.F5M64 1988   358.4'3   88-16644
ISBN 0-13-151374-5

Credits

Editor Ray Bonds
Designer: Philip Gorton
Color artwork: Stephen Seymour, Terry Hadler ©Salamander
Books Ltd.), and © Pilot Press.
Filmset by The Old Mill
Color reproduction by Kentscan Ltd.
Printed in Belgium by Proost International
Book Production, Turnhout.

10 9 8 7 6 5 4 3 2 1

First Prentice Hall Press Edition

The Editor

Ray Bonds is Editorial Director of Salamander Books,
acknowledged as one of the world's leading publishers of
military and defense books. He has written extensively for
defense-related periodicals, and been co-author and/or editor of
more than 80 illustrated books for enthusiasts and serious
military readers alike.

Acknowledgments

The editor would like to thank Bill Gunston for his extensive
contribution to this work. Bill Gunston is a highly respected
defense journalist who has contributed to many international
military and aviation journals. He is the author of numerous
volumes on military aircraft, and is also Assistant Compiler of
Jane's All The World's Aircraft.

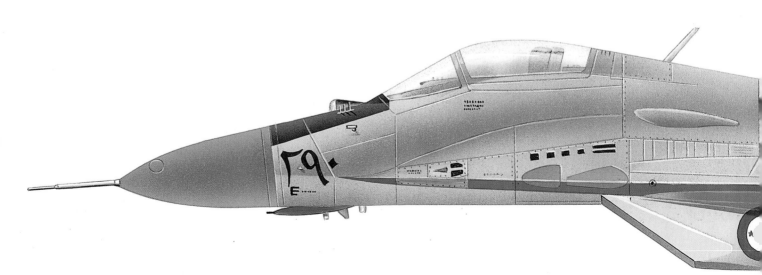

Contents

FIGHTER aircraft today are pressed into so many different roles that the description 'fighter' has become somewhat blurred. There are aircraft called fighters that carry bombs, reconnaissance pods and cameras, as well as the more conventional armament of missiles and guns. There are plenty of small fast combat jets that actually try to avoid tangling with hostile aircraft because their mission is surface attack. There are many trainers that can fly combat missions, such as Britain's 88 Hawk T.1A trainers which are equipped as local-defence fighters.

In deciding which aircraft to include in this book, we have concentrated on dedicated air-to-air combat types, to avoid opening the floodgates to many other warplanes which, Sidewinders and gunpods notwithstanding, are not really what most people understand by the word 'fighter'.

Today we live in an era in which it can take several years for an aircraft design to evolve, and even more years on top of that to complete the test and evaluation programmes. Only by this time may a manufacturer be in a position to go into full-scale production, and then this work may even be carried out by succeeding generations of the original workforce. By the time the aircraft is ready for operational service it is entirely possible that the original requirement has either changed completely or disappeared altogether. It is also possible for a design to be out of date by the time it enters service, since the offensive/defensive capabilities of a rival or potential enemy have evolved at a faster rate.

Many of the aircraft described in this book were originally designed 20, 30 or more years ago, such as the Phantom and some of the MiGs. There are other aircraft included — such as the Eurofighter designs, and Sweden's Gripen — which may not see service with the squadrons until the next decade, or even the next century.

As for the ASTOVL (described later), the initial service date is tentatively put at '2007-2012', which is rather discouraging because the NATO air forces have needed such an aircraft desperately for years in order to have something that can continue to fight on Day 2 of any future war. To accept a wait of a further 15 years seems rather like keeping one's fingers crossed, which most military planners might think an unsound policy!

Of course, most of the blame for the long timescales, and the resulting horrendous costs, can be ascribed to the fact that modern fighters are extremely complicated. One is reminded wistfully of the US Congressman who, during the arguments of 1972-73 concerning Grumman's costs in building the F-14A, exclaimed, "Never again will this nation buy a $20 million fighter!" Everything indicates that his prediction is correct, because most US fighters today cost much more. This is the price we pay for advanced technology.

Whereas, in the past, the technical abilities of a fighter tended to be secondary to the skill of the pilot, today, for better or worse, the technology is dominant. There are now very few active pilots who are experienced in actual combat, and not even the best efforts of USAF's aerial combating training units, the Aggressors, and their Warsaw Pact counterparts, can quite equal the real thing (though it can come remarkably near to it). This certainly does not mean that all pilots are equal — very, very far from it! — but the results of air combat are increasingly likely to be dictated by the hardware.

With regards to the future of air combat an obvious ques-

Below left: Newest cockpit currently in service is that of the F/A-18. Its three coloured multifunction displays are reflected in the vizor.

Below: Impression of how a USAF Advanced Tactical Fighter might look, combining stealth, supercruise and STOL capabilites.

tion to ask is: will there ever come a day when the pilot is merely a passive supervisor, taken along for the ride in case anything happens that a human can cope with but for which the hardware had not been programmed? This leads back to the late 1950s when half the experts thought fighters were being replaced by SAMs and the other half thought they were being replaced by RPVs. Neither of these things has happened, but it is not difficult to argue the case for either. Certainly, in the situation which exists over NATO's Central European front, it seems foolish in the extreme to trade fighters one-for-one against a vastly superior number of enemy aircraft. Far better to use no fighters but large numbers of SAMs, which can unfailingly knock down the enemy on a 1-nil basis without any chance of scoring an unfortunate 'own goal'.

NATO is at present increasingly forced into the dilemma of pretending it can overcome numerical inferiority by technical superiority. Wherever direct measurement is not possible the West makes cosy estimates which seek to prove that Soviet designers are nothing like as clever as those in the West. Their radars may be big, the argument goes, but they are said to be crude, low-powered and short-ranged, and the bigness is explained away as evidence of backwardness. Precisely the same goes for AAMs; for example the AA-6 Acrid is estimated by supposed Western experts to have a range of 23 miles (37km), though it is over 20ft (6m) long and weighs 1,650lb (750kg) while the US Navy's AIM-54 Phoenix flies more than 124 miles (200km) — it is 13ft (4m) long and weighs 1,000lb (450kg). But whenever direct measures are

Above: Though it can fairly be called "the Wright Flyer of STOVL" the little Harrier, represented here by an AV-8A, could survive in a war.

Below: Everyone is excited by the F-16, seen here in two-seat form; but there is no way it could escape destruction on the ground.

possible, as in the case of aircraft guns and numerous army weapons, the notion of in built qualitative superiority vanishes.

If we study the outpourings of the publicity machines of the US manufacturing industry we might conclude that tomorrow's ATFs (Advanced Tactical Fighters) will be souped-up versions of the SR-71, with fuselages about 90ft (27m) long, gross weights in the 100,000lb (45,000kg) class and speeds nudging Mach 3.5. One has only to think for a very few seconds to see that the real future will be very different. First, inflation is already making it extremely hard to build any fighter aircraft at all. Unless we are extremely quick and very clever, as in the case of the F-16, even our small, cheap fighters are going to end up more expensive than the big, capable ones they were intended to replace (the F/A-18A Hornet is an obvious case in point). Second, stealth technology likes small combat aircraft rather than larger ones. Third, anyone who flies at Mach 3.5 needs his head examined; even Mach 2 is almost always nonsense, because it burns fuel quickly, takes time to acheive and eliminates any possibility of inflight manoeuvring.

Fourth, and certainly not the least important, the strange assumption that future wars will be earmarked by dropping a few bombs on runways, leaving "at least 800 metres for all out takeoffs and landings", is as nonsensical as mathematically precise calculations of the percentage of NATO aircraft that would still be operating on Day 3 of an all-out war. The leader of such calculations has for 20 years been the USAF which, because of its power and prestige, exerts a major influence on military thought. However, the fighters described in the following pages are extremely expensive, and many experts consider it an utter waste to have them based on open airfields which are known to be targeted by a potential enemy's land-based missiles. Their view is that, should a major war ever break out, anything based on an airfield will be dead, and that dispersal to thousands of remote operating locations, on land or afloat, is the only apparent way to survive.

Fighter technology

Aircraft design

At the end of World War II fighter designers were in turmoil. All agreed, somewhat prematurely perhaps, that the piston engine was 'out' and that future fighters would have to be jet-propelled. Few had any experience of this new field, and everything was complicated not only by the different installations of such engines but also by the fact that they opened up totally new realms of flight performance, previously not even dreamed of.

This seemed to mean that fighters would have to have new shapes. At first the only 'new shape' was achieved by sweeping back the wings and tail, typically at 30 degrees, and the Korean experience with the F-86 and MiG-15 certainly demonstrated that swept-wing fighters were in a different class from their predecessors. But as jet engines became more powerful, and the performance envelopes expanded further and further, designers continued to feel that they were in uncharted regions. In 1951 the teams that had designed the F-86 and MiG-15 were busy drawing the first fighters able to exceed the speed of sound, Mach 1, in level flight. A mere two years later 'Kelly' Johnson drew performance curves for what became the Lockheed 83 (F-104) and found that with the new J79 engine and properly schemed variable inlets and nozzle the thrust stayed ahead of the drag to beyond Mach 2 (at which point the aircraft was 'redlined' to prevent structural overheating). A mere one year later Mikoyan's team studied the problems of flight at close to 1,553mph (2,500km/h or Mach 2.35), while Republic Aviation was deep in the challenging design of the monster XF-103 fighter to fly at Mach 3.7, or 2,446mph (3,936km/h).

There is no particular technical problem in building a 2,446mph fighter, but such an exercise would not be very useful. Speed is much less important that some people, notably the Dassault company, appear to beleive. The faster an aircraft flies, the greater its radius of turn, because accelerative loading goes up not in proportion to speed but in proportion to the square of the speed. A fighter flying at 2,446 mph flies in a very straight line indeed. If it were to encounter a hostile aircraft it would have to fly right on past it, and take some time to slow down sufficiently to make a reasonable turn. Having allowed the speed to bleed off, it is worse off than the slower aircraft, because the latter (other things being equal) can be smaller, shorter, lighter, cheaper and much more agile.

Prolonged study of the ten years of varied air combat in Southeast Asia in 1963-73 showed that, though afterburners were often used and supersonic speed occasionally reached, every air combat took place at subsonic speed which was usually between 280 and 450 knots. The slower it is possible to fly, the better the rate of turn, to such a degree that missiles able to pull a seemingly impossible 30g at Mach 3 can easily be avoided by a forewarned fighter pulling a mere 3g at 450 knots. When all the variables have been cranked into the fighter design process the answer that emerges is that Mach 2.5 is much faster than the ideal, and a good figure for a rarely attained maximum Mach number is 1.8. This is despite the fact that thanks to superior engines today's fighter has more than twice the thrust that could be packed into the preceding generation.

Even more important than the diminished significance of

Left: Dassault-Breguet's Mirage 2000C typifies the traditional idea of a supersonic high-altitude fighter.

Below: The "performance at all costs" belief led to the F-104A.

Above: Boeing Military Airplane Co built this F-16 mock-up, with a carbonfibre front end, in order to investigate how lightning strikes and big electrical surges might affect future composite structures.

flight speed is the influence of inflation on cost. In World War II a team of 50 draughtsmen in Britain, each earning £5 a week, could turn out hundreds of actual production drawings every week, and complete the design of a fighter in about two months. Today the design of a new fighter needs a team of thousands of engineers, each earning at least £300 a week and doing all sorts of vital things except producing actual drawings of parts.

Eventually hardware does get made, in some cases as the end product of computer graphics and magnetic tape which can steer the machine-tool cutting heads without any ordinary drawing having been created. We have been so busy sitting at our EDP (electronic data processing) graphics terminals in order to save time and work faster that today a new fighter design takes about six years and costs not hundreds of times more but thousands of times more. In a country such as Britain the Air Staff hardly need to bother writing ORs (operational requirements) any more. There is no money to have anything actually built, and if a decision were to be taken to go ahead the OR on which the design was based would be totally outdated years before the first flight of a prototype. Can this truly be regarded as 'progress'.

Aerodynamics

There is, surprisingly, a lot of fashion in aircraft design. Thus, 40 years ago the swept wing was all the rage. Around 35 years ago everyone was excited about deltas (triangular wings). About 25 years ago you were nowhere if you didn't have a VG (variable geometry) 'swing wing', but 15 years ago wings seemed to become ordinary again, seemingly not very different from wings flying during World War II. (In fact, of course, the wings of today's fighters are really marvels of new technology, in both aerodynamics and materials, and the fact that they look 'ordinary' is misleading.)

At the same time, anyone in year 2050 who happens to read this will be stunned that we should think today's wings 'marvels of new technology'. Compared with the wings of birds, or even of insects, they are unbelievably crude. Some have hinged leading or trailing edges, and perhaps some form of blowing system (for example, to keep the flow attached while a flap is depressed to a sharp angle), but apart from this they are unable to change their shape in the slighest. Each shape is correct for only one combination of aircraft weight, air density and Mach number.

The VG swing wing was obviously a very big step forward. In the first production application, the F-111, the upper surface of the fuselage is only gently curved and extremely broad, downstream of leading edges swept at the acute angle of 72.5°. Outboard pivots enable the main outer wings to be swept at this same angle for high-speed flight at mach numbers up to more than 2. For subsonic loiter, and takeoff landing, the wings can be swung forward to only 16° and their lift greatly increased by extending full-span slats and double-slotted flaps.

With the wings spread it is possible to fly relatively slowly yet carry heavy loads, and a major spin off from this is that, if the landing gear is up to it, the aircraft can be flown from short strips with rough surfaces. Variable sweep is obviously good for carrier-based aircraft.

In the high-speed regime the fully swept wing has low wave drag and is close to the ideal for supersonic flight. Its very small span has a further advantage in that a wing of very low aspect ratio, with area distributed mainly from front to rear rather than across a wide span, has what is called a flat lift curve. With ordinary wings the lift varies very sharply indeed with the AOA (angle of attack — the angle at

Below left: Variable-sweep "swing wings", seen here on an F-14, are a powerful way of matching shape to the varying demands.

Below: The F-16A, here in the Netherlands, preferred the simpler scheme of varying wing profile, as shown on the facing page.

F-16 Wing Profiles

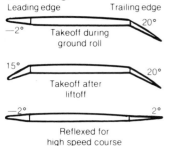

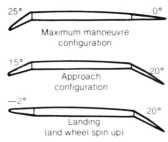

Above: The hinged leading and trailing edges of the F-16's wing can be automatically adjusted to match the wing to different flight regimes. Upward angles have a minus prefix.

Below: Most aeroplanes are designed to be stable, with centre of gravity in front of the centre of wing lift (subsonic on left, supersonic right). CCV (p.13) is the opposite.

Balancing the Conventional Fighter

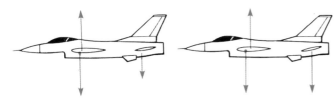

Balancing the CCV (RSS) Fighter

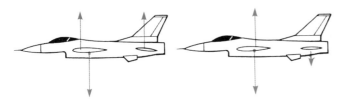

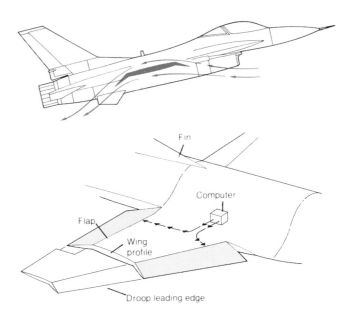

Above: In the F-16 the CCV or RSS (see next page) concept is not taken very far. The computer is not needed to correct the trajectory dozens of times a second but merely to relieve the pilot of the need to keep making intermittent alterations to the wing profile.

which the wing meets the oncoming air), but the ultra-low aspect ratio 'slender wing' shows only small changes in lift over quite large changes in angle of attack. This means a fighter can fly at full throttle through turbulent air close to the ground and hardly respond to the local upcurrents and downcurrents called gusts.

Gust response has been one of the chief factors to consider in designing modern fighter wings, because for 30 years it has been considered that the safest way to penetrate hostile airspace is to fly as low as possible. This gives defenders minimum time to get ready to fire, and in most existing air-defence radars there are technical difficulties in detecting targets very close to the ground. Of course there are problems in flying very low at high speed. As well as the basic need to avoid hitting the ground, the mission range is greatly reduced because gas-turbine engines burn fuel several times faster at low level than in the very cold thin air at high altitude, and the density of the air greatly increases the stresses imposed on the aircraft structure. A very real difficulty in most regions is birdstrikes; no matter how well aircraft are designed to withstand impacts with birds, severe birdstrikes can kill the pilot, damage a tailplane enough to cause an immediate dive into the ground, or simply wreck the engine or block up the air inlet(s).

Apart from this, the problem of gust response is a limiting factor in what a human crew can stand, especially in the crucial case of maximum speed at the lowest level. People who are not combat aircrew may not appreciate that gust response translates into bone-crushing, eyeball-jerking movements in the vertical plane which also have the effect of eating into airframe fatigue life. The smooth ride of the VC aircraft is not just a matter of comfort but of being able to fly the mission properly.

In designing the F-16, and to a lesser extent the F/A-18, the wing was given some VG capability by fitting full-span leading-edge droops and large trailing edge flaps. Computer-controlled, these adjust the profile of the wing to suit takeoff, cruise, high-g manoeuvres, supersonic flight and landing.

The ideal, of course, is a wing made of flexible material whose section profile and planform shape can all be varied continuously, and this is certainly beyond the present state of the art. The best that is practicable is to make the wing what the Americasn call 'mission adaptive' by changing its profile and, if possible, planform shape, in easy stages by providing it with various kinds of hinges and pivots. The best answer for each aircraft is a compromise between performance, complexity, cost and reliability, like most things in aviation.

There are many other aspects of fighter aerodynamics. Slender wings in which roof chord exceeds the span can fly at angles of attack far beyond those at which ordinary wings stall. Fly an F-14 with the wings outspread, and you have a conventional aeroplane with a wing that stalls at around 16 degrees AOA, despite help from slats and flaps. Sweep the wing to 68 degree and in extreme conditions you can fly at AOA from 60 degree to beyond 90 degree; the same applies to many other fighters. It is doubtful that today's designers are working on a single fighter that cannot routinely fly at AOA greater than 60 degrees in air-combat manoeuvres.

Ability to fly routinely at such incredible AOA is part of what is today called 'carefree manoeuvring', which means that the pilot can try to make his mount do 'impossible' manoeuvres but will never induce loss of control or a 'departure', such as flicking into a high-speed stall and spin, which would be lethal at low level and in fact caused many F-4Cs and Ds to crash in Vietnam. Not only this, but modern fighters are designed with full knowledge of CCV (control-configured vehicle) technology. Here the fighter is deliberately designed without natural flight stability, the buzzword being RSS (relaxed static stability). As soon as it tries to fly, such an aircraft will attempt to swap ends, but such a motion would be instantly sensed by the flight control system and countered by split-second deflection of the control surfaces to keep the aircraft flying point-first.

CCV fighters rely totally upon the instantaneous reaction of their computerized flight control sensors and the only

Left: Experimental carbonfibre/epoxy wing skins, with integral stiffeners. These offer better ratio of strength and stiffness to mass, and can be tailored so that the structure bends and twists in the most favourable way.

Below: Over 90 per cent of the surface of the HiMat is carbonfibre. HiMat is a Rockwell/USAF research programme exploring realms of air combat manoeuvrability previously unknown. Two have flown.

slightly slower deflections of their powered control surfaces. They are in principle like a dart whose flights have been taken from the tail and mounted on the point, and then put under the control of a fast-acting control system to keep the dart flying the right way round.

A CCV engineer in British Aerospace said that the task of the control system is exactly that of a man sitting on the bonnet of a 60mph car and pushing a bicycle back-to-front, steering it by the handlebars. Ordinary humans would lose control of such a bicycle at speeds greater than about 3mph (almost 5km/h), but the CCV flight controls react fast enough to keep it running accurately at 60mph (96.56km/h). There might be 100 movements each second, each too small to be noticed.

CCV aircraft may not look unusual, but they have their CG (centre of gravity) far to the rear. Two aircraft which have penetrated well into the CCV domain are the F-16 and mirage 2000. Such aircraft need FBW (fly by wire) electrically signalled flight controls, fast-acting surface power units, highly reliable and multi-redundant flight-control systems (typically with two pairs of hydraulic power systems and electric signalling so that any fault is countered by a 3-over-1 or 2-0 majority) and a new order of on-board EDP able to use much more flight information at much higher speed. The CCV fighter not only has potentially more rapid power of manoeuvre but can be made smaller, lighter and more efficient in many other ways.

Right: If it were made by all-metal stressed-skin methods the wing of *the Grumman X-29 FSW would be torn off in high-speed manoeuvres.*

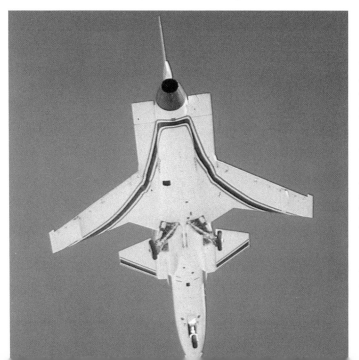

Structure

Until the 1960s aluninium and its alloys was used for virtually 100 per cent of the airframe of all fighters. A few aberrations outside the mainstream of fighter development used mainly steel (MiG-25) or titanium (SR-71), while the development of very strong and stiff yet lightweight fibres of carbon/graphite or boron has increasingly led to the use of FRC (fibre-reinforced composites) in components where GRP (glass reinforced plastics) might be equally strong but insufficiently stiff. Unlike typical metals in practical polycrystalline bulk, the new composite materials exhibit undirectional stiffness. In other words a sheet, for example, can be made flexible in one direction and extremely rigid in another. By choosing the directions of the stiff reinforcing fibres it is possible to create structures unlike any that were previously possible, able to bend in exactly the way the designer wishes.

Nobody is benefiting more from this than the designers of fighter aircraft. previously a wing had to be made stiff, because if in a tight turn or dive pull-out it bent excessively the changed angle of incidence of the outer sections could cause what is called aeroelastic divergence. The bending would turn the wing to a greater angle to the airflow, and the suddenly increased air load could then bend the wing still further, and so on until the wing ripped off, the whole process occupying a small fraction of a second. It was for this reason that the FSW (forward-swept wing) could never be used, even though it was recognised as early as 1944 as better than the swept-back wing in almost every respect.

The FSW offers lower drag at almost all Mach numbers; therefore a fighter can have a smaller engine burning less fuel, which in turn reduces gross weight, so the wing can be smaller, and so on in a favourable circle of interacting effects. The FSW offers greater manoeuvrablity at all speeds, better handling at low speeds, and lower stalling speed under good control, and thus reduced runway requirements. The FSW fighter can be made virtually spinproof, and certainly can be smaller and cheaper than any alternative shape.

This is really an aerodynamic argument, but it is covered here because the realization of the FSW has been entirely due to new composite structures. These can be made so stiff, using skins reinforced with graphite fibres laid in appropriate directions, that the previously impossible FSW can be flown up to supersonic speeds and pulled into tight turns without the spectre of sudden divergence pulling the wings off.

Grumman designed the first FSW aircraft, the X-29A, which first flew in December 1984. it has a powered hinged trailing edge to give variable camber and a close-coupled foreplane for use as a primary flight control and to provide the necessary nose-up trim in the supersonic regime by an upward force, instead of by a downward force as is required by aircraft with trimming surfaces at the rear.

Another American research aircraft for future fighters is the Rockwell HiMAT (highly manoeuvrable aircraft technology). This is a pilotless RPV (remotely piloted vehicle), powered by the same J85 afterburning turbojet as used in the twin-engined F-5E. Its wing and large canards are aero-elastically tailored so that, as they deflect upwards in tight manoeuvres, the angle of incidence does not increase but decrease. This is done by making the main structural parts of these surfaces out of graphite composite sheets with the plies oriented at carefully chosen angles, mainly diagonal, to control the change of the airfoil shape under severe loads. Again, HiMAT has mechanical camber change along leading and trailing edges.

For structural as well as aerodynamic reasons previous fighter canards have been used only as a trimming device or to enhance takeoff and landing and low-speed handling. Many, such as those of the Krif and Mirage 2000, are mere fixed surfaces. On the HiMAT, two of which are flying, the canards have elevators and are used in conjunction with the variable-camber main wing to enhance agility throughout the entire flight envelope which extends to Mach 1.6 HiMAT has no fragile pilot and its positive g-limit is a bonecrushing + 12, though the normal manoeuvring limit is a sustained turn at 8g at Mach 0.9 at 30,000ft (9,145m). Only 25 per cent of the present structure is light allow, other percentages being: graphite composite 25, titanium 19, steel 9, glass-fibre 4, all other materials 18.

Weapons

just as the advent of the turbojet made many people jump to the conclusion that propellers were obsolete, so did the advent of the SAM (surface-to-air missile) lead some important people in Britain to the conclusion that all manned fighters were obsolete. Another of these crassly simplistic beliefs stemmed from the invention of the AAM (air-to-air missile), which by the late 1950s had convinced many experts that fighter guns were obsolete. There are plenty of fat treatises on fighter armament dating from that period which ignore the gun completely, the only alternative to the AAM considered being the spin-stabilized rocket. The authors of those documents did not have the slightest indication that by 1965 the CO of the USAF 8th Tactical Fighter Wing in Vietnam would say publicly, "A fighter without a gun is like a bird without a wing."

Britain's RAF gradually recovered from the belief that it would need no more fighters, but no internal gun was asked for in the P.1154 Mach-2 V/STOL nor in the Phantom which replaced it, and the RAF's Phantom often has to carry a 20mm SUU-23A gun pod on the centreline pylon.

Fundamentally, the use of an external gun pod is undesirable unless it is known that a gun will seldom be needed. It sterilizes a pylon, invariably upsets aircraft trim when firing and makes accuracy unattainable.

There was great activity among Allied gun designers when they discovered the progress made in the technology by Germany during World War II. A dramatic breakthrough came in 1951-3 with the development of the six-barrel Vulcan, produced by GE mainly as the 20mm M61. It is as if six wartime 20mm cannon had been combined in one gun and fed with vast amounts of ammunition for a giant drum, in recent installations with a linkless feed system. The gun proved so effective it has been virtually standard on US fighters for over 25 years. In many installations (F-104, F-105, F-14, F-15, F-16) it has been well to one side of the centreline, where it at first kicked the aim off-target, though in today's fighters it automatically calls up rudder deflection via the computerized flight-control system.

What we know of Soviet gun development suggests that there has been steady and carefully considered development, whereas Britain's relatively tiny RAF now finds itself with guns of 20mm, 25mm, 27mm and 30mm calibre, which surely cannot have been intended? Moreover, alone among modern air forces, the British Air Staff cannot see any reason for a gun inEFA (there is no gun in EAP, but that might not of itself mean very much). The British view is that 'if they get within gun firing range, something is very wrong'. This is just what everyone was saying 30 years ago. One can only hope the RAF will not have to learn the error of its ways 'the hard way'.

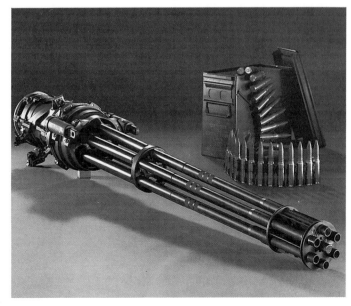

Above: Looking up at an F/A-18A, showing one of the many possible weapon loads: four Mk 83 bombs and two AIM-9L Sidewinders. Also on board are three tanks and two Lantirn pods for low flying at night, while under the nose can be seen the gun-bay gas vents.

Left: An armourer at RAF Brüggen checks over the feed conveyor for the 20mm ammunition in a General Electric SUU-23/A pod under a Phantom FGR.2. This pod enables the gunless aircraft to carry an M61 six-barrel "Gatling gun".

Right: Here shown with 20mm ammunition for comparison, the General Electric M61A-1 has for over 30 years been virtually a standard fit on American fighters. Apart from very high rate of fire (normally 4,000 or 6,000 rds/min) it is extremely reliable.

Missiles

It is difficult to avoid being equally concerned at the failure of the NATO alliance to come up with any kind of plan for AAMs (air-to-air missiles).The ability of US industry, notably Ford Aerospace, to keep improving the Sidewinder has at least put progressively better close-range dogfight weapons in the hands of troops, but Sidewinder itself is now over 30 years old. All that has been done over this period is to bolt on better nose guidance sections and control canards, and fit an improved smokeless motor in the tube at the rear, and in the all-aspect AIM-9L and 9M to incorporate a much better ABF (annular blast fragmentation) warhead. Basic aerodynamics have hardly altered, and in any case the need to provide IR (infra-red, or heat) homing guidance or semi-active radar homing as a direct alternative has been consistently abandoned.

A semi-active radar missile flies towards the reflections from the target of radar signals transmitted by the fighter. The target, as seen by the missile, tends to be rather diffuse and variable, because the centroid (the apparent geometrical centre) keeps changing according to the target's attitude and other factors.

In contrast an IR missile sees only the hottest parts of the target, in particular the hot metal of the jetpipe or, better still, the final turbine stage as seen up the jetpipe (best of all, by far, is an operative afterburner). All-aspect IR missiles have particularly sensitive seeker heads which can unfailingly lock-on to the target aircraft regions which are only slightly hotter than the ambient background. Cunning filters and electronics are needed to prevent the missile from ever

IR homing AAM
Sidewinder

These simplified diagrams show the basic principles used in the two commonest forms of air-to-air missile today. The heat (IR) homer is passive; the fighter that launched it can at once leave it to home on the IR radiated from the target. In contrast the semi-active radar homer relies upon the fighter continuing to fly towards the enemy in order to "illuminate" it with its nose radar (blue beam).

Semi-active radar guidance
Sparrow

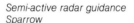

Below: When AIM-120A AMRAAM (seen here on an F-15) gets into service it will multiply the effectiveness of most Western fighters.

Below: One of today's most formidable fighters is the Soviet MiG-29, picked by India after evaluating six competing types. This is carrying four small R-60 dogfight missiles, two big "AA-10 Alamo-A" missiles (notable for reverse-taper control fins) and a large drop tank.

locking-on to either the Sun or ground reflections, such as from lakes and rivers.

In general the only difference between radar and IR is one of wavelength, IR having a very much shorter wavelength close to that of visible light. Short wavelength can mean a more precise picture (for example, if we ourselves saw at radio/radar wavelengths we should have a very poor view indeed, compared with the fantastically rich picture we actually enjoy), but it also means rapid attenuation due to scattering of the energy by rain, atmospheric moisture, dust, fog, cloud and similar phenomena. In a tropical rainstorm the effective range of a Sidewinder would be measured in feet rather than miles.

It is extraordinary that, though there have been several studies for radar Sidewinders, and the AIM-9C was put into production (chiefly for the F-8 Crusader), every Sidewinder in service has IR guidance only. So do the French Magic, and Israel's Shafrir and Python 3.

In contrast, every known Soviet AAM is in service with a choice of radar or IR homing, and the usual load is pairs of missiles, one of each. This gives the greatest lethality according to the weather and other conditions, and also doubles the spread of wavelengths over which the enemy must provide countermeasures.

For the longest range of all there is no practical alternative to active homing, usually using radar wavelengths (though the missile could use IR or laser wavelengths). In active homing the missile itself emits the radiation that is reflected from the target, and the reason for adopting this method will be appreciated when it is remembered that emitted energy, such as radio or heat waves, falls away not in proportion to the distance but in proportion to the square of the distance.

An F-14 Tomcat can pick out an enemy aircraft at a typical distance of 125 miles (200km), even if the target is seen almost nose-on. To do this the radar waves have to travel 250 miles (400km), because they have to go to the target and then be reflected back to the F-14. Compared with the situation at 1¼ miles (2km) range, this means the recieved signals are 10,000 times weaker! This would be asking rather a lot of the miniaturized guidance in an F-14's Phoenix missile, so to begin with the missile is merely fired in the direction of the target, flying on autopilot (which in the new AIM-54C version is a strapdown inertial unit). When it gets near the target the missile's own radar is switched on, the planar-array scanner searches and locks-on, and thereafter the missile homes on the reflections of its own radar.

Until the 1960s it was very difficult for fighters to intercept aircraft flying close to the ground. The land or sea tends to act as a giant reflector of radar waves, to that seaching from above for an intruder at tree top height is pointless; the small reflection is lost against the overall reflection from the ground. It took prolonged research, by no means all in the United States despite a common American belief, to produce 'overland downlook' radars. Cunning computers and software in modern radars can process and manage the signals in such a way that all reflections from the Earth's surface, or all reflections from stationary objects, are eliminated. Thus the display in the cockpit looks blank except for items that are moving or which are well above ground level.

Left: An unusual view of an F-14A about to land on USS Saratoga in 1986. It is carrying four Sparrows, four Sidewinders and two tanks.

Below: The RAF's Tornado interceptor carries four Sky Flash missiles recessed under the fuselage, plus Sidewinders on the tank pylons.

Above: Dassault-Breguet's Rafale will carry Super 530 and/or MICA missiles under the fuselage and wings, and a 30mm gun.

Below: Another example of Lockheed's high-quality Advanced Tactical Fighter art. But how can white-hot afterburners be stealthy?

Fighters of the Future

Even in the welcome new openness of *Glasnost* we cannot expect to know much about the new fighter designs being developed in the Soviet Union, but we may be certain that they will be able to do everything asked of them. Even today the MiG-29 and Su-27 are in many ways outstanding, yet, paradoxically, both strongly resemble American studies of the late 1960s which led to the F-14 and F-15.

In some parts of the world the fashionable idea for tomorrow's fighter is a rather close-coupled machine with a canard foreplane in front of a broad delta (triangular) wing, with inlets under the fuselage. After toying with inclined twin vertical tails (if that is not self-contradictory) designers now think a single fin is fashionable, and the new designs in Israel and Sweden are commendably small machines with only one engine. New fighters are also being developed in India (LCA, light combat aircraft) and Yugoslavia (Novi Avion),

could perhaps become the world's major exporter of fighters by the year 2000.

Right at the other end of the scale, and unlikely to be afforded by any country except the United States, is the ATF (advanced tactical fighter). Together with the Northrop Advanced Technology Bomber, this has been the US Air Force's top priority programme for several years. A vast amount of research and engineering effort has gone into its possible aerodynamics, materials, structure, propulsion, cockpit, avionics, weapons and tactical operation. It has been said that the ATF must be capable of taking off and landing on cratered runways (a basic idea that anyone with imagination might consider nonsensical), crusing at supersonic speed without using afterburners, of achieving unrivalled inflight agility, carrying the most advanced avionics and weapons and get being designed from the start as a totally 'low-observable' or 'stealth' aircraft.

Most of the big names in the US industry fought to win this potentially huge programme, with 750 aircraft (probably costing $50-$100 million each) for the USAF, plus a potential 550 of a navalized version to replace the F-14. In October 1986 two types were picked, the Lockheed YF-22A, assisted by General Dynamics and Boeing, and the Northrop YF-23A, assisted by McDonnell Douglas. The candidate engines, both advanced augmented turbofans, are the Pratt & Whitney YF119 and the General Electric YF120. Prototypes of each fighter are to fly with both types of engine. From the start, tremendous efforts have been made to ensure that the ATF will be able to serve for over 20 years with the highest degree of reliablity and availability and the lowest total cost of ownership. The programme has always been intensely competitive, and calls for the utmost skill in programme management.

The ASTOVL (advanced short vertical take off and landing) is much more nebulous, though it has been desperately needed for many years. Whereas ATF prototypes are to fly in 1989, no ASTOVL is expected to fly until the next century, and it might be after 2005 before it reaches user squadrons. This is in part because nobody yet knows how it should best be designed. It could have a simple vectored-thrust engine, like a Harrier. It could have an augmentor ejector, in which bleed air blasts down through gaint ducts to entrain fresh airflow for lift. It could use the RALS (remote augmented lift system) in which bleed air feeds a separate jet with combustion chamber near the nose, or it could have a tandem-fan engine with various valves and deflector doors. The trouble is that each concept seems to be better than the others — though surely commonsense suggests building quickly on known Harrier technology and having an advanced vectored-thrust aircraft in service in the shortest time possible?

Above: BAe were told their P.1214-3 advanced STOVL project may be brilliant, but the RAF wants to be tied to airfields.

Below: This project by Dornier, assisted by Northrop, typically combines agility with the need for a (short) runway.

and it will be interesting to see if these also are single-engined. Certainly the Swedes, whose Gripen is included in this book, are to be congratulated on acheiving all their targets for multirole capability within a 'normal maximum takeoff weight' of only 17,635lb (8,000kg) . This translates directly in to low cost, both to buy the aircraft and top operate it, and if Sweden was not so dedicatedly neutral it

BAe Sea Harrier

After years of delay the Sea Harrier at last got the go-ahead in May 1975. It was developed from the Harrier chiefly by redesigning the forward fuselage. The deeper structure provides for a Ferranti Blue Fox radar, which folds 180° for shipboard stowage, and a new cockpit with the seat raised to provide space for a much-enhanced nav/attack/combat system and to give an all-round view.

The Royal Navy purchased 24, plus a further 10, FRS.1s, the designation meaning 'fighter reconnaissance strike'. In the NATO context the main task is air defence, normally with direction from surface vessels, either as DLI (deck-launched intercept) or CAP (combat air patrol).

In the Falklands fighting these aircraft repeatedly demonstrated their ability to fly six sorties a day in extremely severe weather, with maintenance by torchlight at night often in hail blizzards. Serviceability was consistently around 95 per cent each morning. CAPs were flown at 10,000ft (3,000m) at 290mph (463km/h), and within a few seconds it was possible to be closing on an enemy at 690mph (1,1100km/h) just above the sea; 24 Argentine aircraft were claimed by AIM-9L Sidewinders and seven by guns. New techniques were demonstrated, including 4,000-mile (6,440km) flights to land on ships'(sometimes by pilots who had never landed on a ship), and operations from sheet laid on containers in a merchant ship.

Above: A pair of Sea Harriers from No 801 Sqn, HMS Invincible. The nearer aircraft destroyed a Mirage and a Dagger in 1982.

Right: The Spanish Navy operates these US-supplied AV-8A Harriers and now (described on a later page) the later AV-8B Harrier II.

Nearer to Europe, the Sea Harrier is envisaged as filling the fleet defensive band between ship-to-air missiles and F-14s with Phoenix AAMs. Its ESM fit is more advanced than that of land-based Harriers, and is used as a primary aid to intercept aircraft or sea-skimming missiles. Pilots normally operate as individuals, flying any mission for which they are qualified.

Left: In order to fit the cramped British ships the Blue Fox nose radar folds through 180°. The FRS.2 will have the bigger Blue Vixen.

Below; XZ457 is shown serving with No 899, the training unit at RNAS Yeovilton. Kill markings show two Mirages and a Skyhawk in 1982.

Origin: United Kingdom.
Engine: One Rolls-Royce Pegasus 104 rated at 21,500lb (9,752kg).
Dimensions: Span 25ft 3in (7.7m); length 47ft 7in (14.5m); height 12ft 2in (3.71m); wing area 201.1ft² (18.68m²).
Weights: Empty 14,052lb (6,374kg); max 26,200lb (11,880kg).
Performance: Max speed over 737mph (1,186km/h); typical lo attack speed 690mph (1,110km/h); hi intercept radius (3min combat plus reserves and vertical landing) 460 miles (750km); lo strike radius 288 miles (463km).
Armament: Two 30mm Aden Mk 4 each with 150 rounds; five hardpoints for max weapon load of 8,000lb (3,630kg) including Sea Eagle or Harpoon ASMs, Sidewinder AAMs and other stores.
History: First flight 20 August 1978; service delivery 18 June 1979.

By the middle of 1984 23 additional aircraft had been ordered to increase the establishment of the three combat squadrons, 800, 801 and 809 — normally embarked aboard *Invincible, Illustrious* and *Ark Royal* — and the training unit, 899, at Yeovilton.

Under a mid-life improvement programme the aircraft are to be updated to have a lookdown-shootdown capability with a new radar the Ferranti Blue Vixen. This will match the range of the Sea Eagle. Wing tips and rear fuselage will be extended, new avionics fitted together with four AIM-120A (AMRAAM) AAMs, and the cockpit will be updated.

The Indian Navy purchased six FRS.51s and two T.60 two-seat trainers, followed by a repeat order for ten Mk 51s and one trainer. They operate with No 300 Sqn from shore bases and from INS *Vikrant*. Eight further aircraft have been ordered, following the transfer of *Hermes* to the Indian Navy as INS *Viraat*.

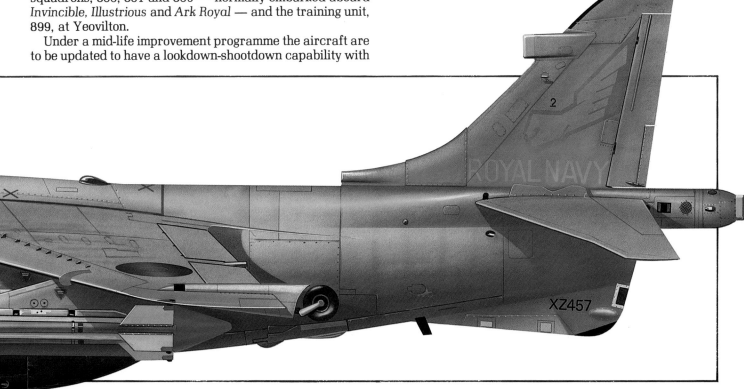

Dassault-Breguet Mirage III

The most commercially successful fighter ever built in Western Europe, the tailless delta Mirage had the advantage of proven combat success in 1967 with Israel, the first export customer, and this catapulted it into the limelight and brought about sales of 1,410 to 20 air forces.

Most of today's aircraft are variants of the IIIE fighter-bomber or the 5, a simplified model without radar and able to carry additional fuel or bombs. Like all early tailless deltas they need a long runway and cannot make sustained turns without speed bleeding off. The Mirage was planned to operate from rough strips, but the tyre pressure combined with high take-off and landing speeds make this a rare occurrence.

Some customers have bought dual trainers, others the IIIR with a camera-filled nose (South Africa's R2Z having the uprated 9K-50 engine, and the chin bulge showing the installation of doppler). Chile bought the final model, the 50, and these have been updated with canards by Israel.

Some customers, such as Peru, have updated their Mirages using kits for a HUD, inertial navigation system, laser ranger and Magic AAMs, and the update market for Mirage deltas is a major one. In Switzerland and in France, canard foreplanes are being fitted to add more manoeuvrability in combat.

Below: Four F-103s of the Forca Aérea Brasileira. F-103 is the Brazilian designation for the Mirage IIIEBR, a typical sub-type of the IIIE.

Foot of page: One of 39 tandem dual-control Mirage IIIB trainers flying with France's Armée de l'Air. They are longer than the single-seaters.

Origin: France.
Engine: (Most) one SNECMA Atar 9C turbojet rated at 13,670lb (6,200kg); (IIIR2Z, NG and 50) 15,873lb (7,200kg) Atar 9K50.
Dimensions: Span 27ft (8.22m); length (IIIE) 49ft 3½in (15.03m), (5) 51ft 0¼in (15.55m); height 13ft 11½in (4.25m); wing area 375ft² (35.0m²).
Weights: Empty (IIIE) 15,540lb (7,050kg), (5) 14,550lb (6,600kg); loaded (IIIE 5) 29,760lb (13,500kg).
Performance: Max speed (clean) 870mph (1,400km/h, Mach 1.14) at sea level, 1,450mph (2,335km/h, Mach 2.2) at altitude; initial climb 16,400ft (5,000m)/min, service ceiling 55,775ft (17,000m); combat radius in attack mission with two bombs and tanks (hi-altitude) 745 miles (1,200km).
Armament: Two 30mm DEFA 5-52 cannon, each with 125 rounds; three 1,000lb (454kg) pylons for bombs, missiles or tanks, (Mirage 5) seven pylons with max capacity of 9,260lb (4,200kg).
History: First flight (prototype Mirage III-001) 17 November 1956, (production IIIC) 9 October 1960, (prototype 5) 19 May 1967.

Right: Mirage IIIC with ADF dorsal fin, twin-eyelid nozzle and rocket (far right) typical IIIE tail.

Left: Looking down on a Mirage IIIE of France's Armée de l'Air. The airbrakes can be seen painted red/yellow.

Right: Looking up at the French IIIE shown above. The weapons are an AS 37 Martel anti-radar missile and two Matra Magic dogfight AAMs.

The first production version, the Mirage IIIC, had a shorter nose and less fuel than subsequent versions. It was supplied to France, Israel and S. Africa.

Dassault-Breguet Mirage F1

The F1 has a wing much smaller than the deltas but so efficient that the aircraft has shorter field length, slower landing, and (with 40 per cent greater internal fuel) three times the supersonic endurance, or twice the tactical radius at low level, with superior manoeuvrability.

L'Armée de l'Air achieved operational F.1C capability with 30e Escadre at Reims, followed by 5e Escadre at Orange, whose three squadrons include 25 of the F1.C-200 type with FR probes for deployment to Djibouti, 3,100 miles, (5,000km) away, and EC 12 at Cambrai.

Equipped with Cyrano IV radar and Magic and Super 530 AAMs, the F1.C is a capable interceptor. Most customers have bought an EW suite including the Type BF RWR. In a few air forces, the Remora self-protection jammer is carried, and in the ECM role the usual jammer is the powerful Caiman. Most export customers have matched the F1 with the relatively cheap Magic dogfight AAM. Recently the Mle 30-791B gun has become available, firing higher-

Above: One of the first production Mirage F1.Cs prior to delivery. Note the perforated spoilers above the wings and the tip Magic AAMs.

Below: Seen here serving with the famed Normandie-Niemen unit, the F1.C-200 is distinguished by having a fixed flight-refuelling probe.

performance 30mm ammunition at 2,500rds/min.

There are four basic sub-variants. Most have been derived from the F1.C with radar, and this family includes the F1.E multirole model with inertial navigation, a central computer and a HUD. The F1.A is a simplified model with a slim, non-radar nose, configured mainly for ground attack; the F1.B is a trainer with combat capability but reduced fuel; and the F1.R is a dedicated reconnaissance version with internal cameras and other sensors.

Origin: France.
Engine: One SNECMA Atar 9K-50 rated at 15,873lb (7,200kg).
Dimensions: Span 27ft 6¾ in (8.4m); length (F1.C) 49ft 2½ in (15m); height (F.1C) 14ft 9in (4.5m); wing area 269.1ft² (25m²).
Weights: Empty (F1.C) 16,314lb (7,400kg), (F1.E) 17,857lb (8,100kg); loaded (max) (F1.C) 32,850lb (14,900kg), (F1.E) 33,510lb (15,200kg).
Performance: Max speed (clean) 910mph (1,470km/h, Mach 1.2) at sea level, 1,450mph (2,335km/h, Mach 2.2) at altitude; initial climb (F1.C) 41,930–47,835ft (12,780-14,580m)/min; service ceiling (F1.C) 65,600ft (20,000m); range with max weapons (hi-lo-hi) (F1.C) 560 miles (900km).
Armament: (Both versions) Two 30mm DEFA 5-53 cannon, each with 135 rounds; five pylons, total weapon load 8,820lb (4,000kg).
History: First flight 23 December 1966, service delivery 14 March 1973.

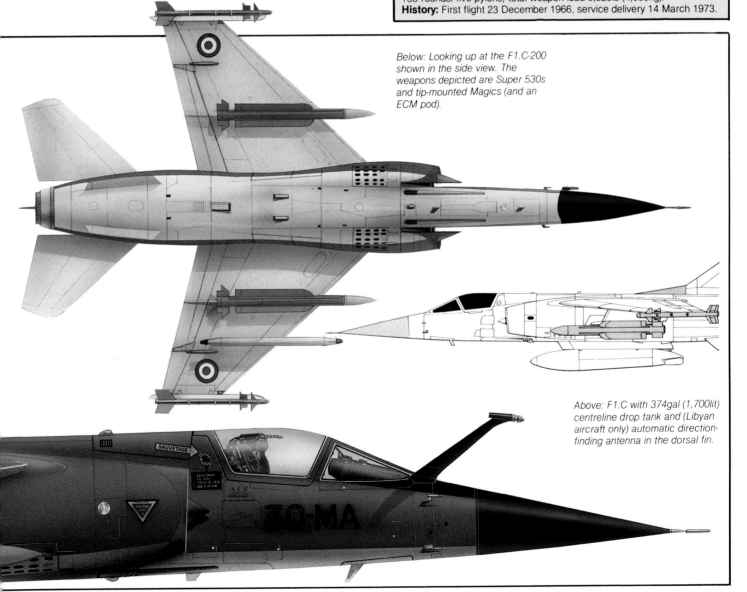

Below: Looking up at the F1.C-200 shown in the side view. The weapons depicted are Super 530s and tip-mounted Magics (and an ECM pod).

Above: F1.C with 374gal (1,700lit) centreline drop tank and (Libyan aircraft only) automatic direction-finding antenna in the dorsal fin.

Dassault-Breguet Mirage 2000

Very strongly biased to the air superiority mission, the 2000 was made possible by the emergence of CCV (control configured vehicle) technology which by combining FBW (fly-by-wire) signalling with instant-action computer control and multilane channel redundancy allows a fighter to be made basically unstable. The wing has leading-edge flaps which provide controlled camber for use in different flight regimes.

Early Mirage 2000s were powered by the M53-2, but production machines have the M53-5. In 1985 deliveries began of the M53-P2, with a thrust of 21,360lb (9,689kg). This powers the 2000N and some export customers have also specified the P2. A flight-refuelling probe can be attached.

Most customers see their Mirage 2000s purely as air-combat aircraft, though the radar-guided Super 530D AAM matched to the RDI pulse-doppler radar has yet to be exported and the radar itself has been delayed. Thus the RDM radar, a simplified earlier set, is fitted to most current Mirage 2000s.

The 2000N (*nucléaire*) is a two-seater stressed to fly at 690mph (1,110km/h) at low altitude whilst carrying an ASMP missile. It has an Antilope V terrain-following radar, two inertial platforms, a colour display in the cockpit and improved ECM.

Dassault-Breguet has gained several export contracts. Egypt has ordered 16 2000EMs and four two-seat BMs, all with the P2 engine. India bought 40 (36 2000H and four 2000TH trainers, most with the Dash-5 engine), named Vajra (Divine Thunder). Abu Dhabi has ordered 36 (22 EAD, six DAD trainers and eight of an RAD reconnaissance version). Peru planned to order 26, but to save 'over $500 million' cut the order back to 12. Greece is buying 36 2000EG single-seaters and four 2000BG trainers. Jordan is buying 12.

Below: A test firing of an Aérospatiale AS 30L laser-guided attack missile. Most 2000Cs are used primarily for air-superiority.

Origin: France.
Engine: One SNEĆMA M53-5 rated at 19,840lb (9,000kg).
Dimensions: Span 29ft 6in (9.0m); length 47ft 1in (14.35m); height 17ft 6in (5.3m); wing area 441ft² (41m²).
Weights: Empty 16,315lb (7,400kg); normal take-off, air-intercept mission 33,000lb (14,969kg); max 36,375lb (16,500kg).
Performance: Max speed at 36,000ft (11,000m) 1,320mph (2,124km/h, Mach 2.2); max at low level 690mph (1,110km/h); range (two tanks) over 1,118 miles (1,800km).
Armament: Two 30mm DEFA 5-53 cannon; normal air-intercept load two Matra Super 530 and two Matra 550 Magic AAMs; (2000N) one ASMP cruise missile, able to carry a 150-kilotonne warhead up to 62 miles (100km).
History: First flight 10 March 1978; production delivery December 1983.

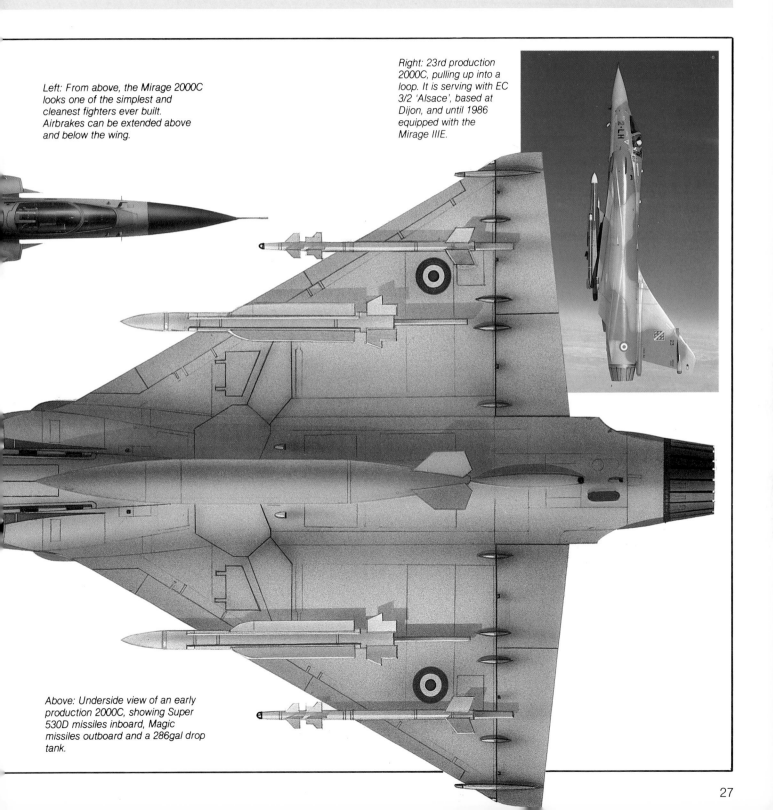

Left: From above, the Mirage 2000C looks one of the simplest and cleanest fighters ever built. Airbrakes can be extended above and below the wing.

Right: 23rd production 2000C, pulling up into a loop. It is serving with EC 3/2 'Alsace', based at Dijon, and until 1986 equipped with the Mirage IIIE.

Above: Underside view of an early production 2000C, showing Super 530D missiles inboard, Magic missiles outboard and a 286gal drop tank.

Dassault-Breguet Rafale

Origin: France.
Specification for prototype:
Engines: Two General Electric F404-400s rated at 16,000lb (7,258kg).
Dimensions: Span (over empty missile pylons) 36ft 9in (11.2m); length 51ft 10in (15.8m); height 17ft (5.18m); wing area 506ft² (47m²).
Weights: Empty equipped 20,940lb (9,500kg); combat weight (4 Mica and 2 Magic AAMs) 30,865lb (14,000kg); max loaded 44,090lb (20,000kg).
Performance: Max speed (clean, hi-altitude) 1,320mph (2,135km/h, Mach 2); (sea level) 920mph (1,480km/h); combat radius 400 miles (644km).
Armament: One 30mm gun; pylons for attack load of 7,715lb (3,500kg) or up to six air-defence missiles (typically four Mica and two Magic).
History: First flight 4 July 1986; operational service date 1996.

Today's Rafale (Squall) is the technology demonstrator intended to underpin the Rafale D for l'Armée de l'Air and the Rafale M for l'Aéronavale.

Features include a rear wing and close-coupled canards, digital avionics with quadruply redundant FBW (fly-by-wire) flight controls, a Martin-Baker Mk 10 seat inclined back at 30–40°, sidestick controller, large holographic HUD, multifunction displays, and voice-activated pilot inputs.

Most of the wings, foreplane and vertical tail are of carbon fibre, the wing root fairings and wing tips are of Kevlar, the air-inlet ducts are of aluminium-lithium alloy and the slats are of superplastic-formed titanium. Wing camber can naturally be varied under computer control throughout each flight to achieve the highest possible manoeuvrability with 'carefree' handling.

Serge Dassault said in July 1986 that the company was 'prepared to consider possible co-operation from outside Europe'. The Rafale D and M will have wing area reduced to 474ft² (44m²), cutting empty weight to 18,960lb (8,600kg). The engines are expected to be new French turbofans derived from the SNECMA M88.

The company sees itself as being in head-on competition with EuroFighter GmbH in an attempt to win markets throughout the world estimated to encompass 'at least 1,000 aircraft' excluding the original developing country.

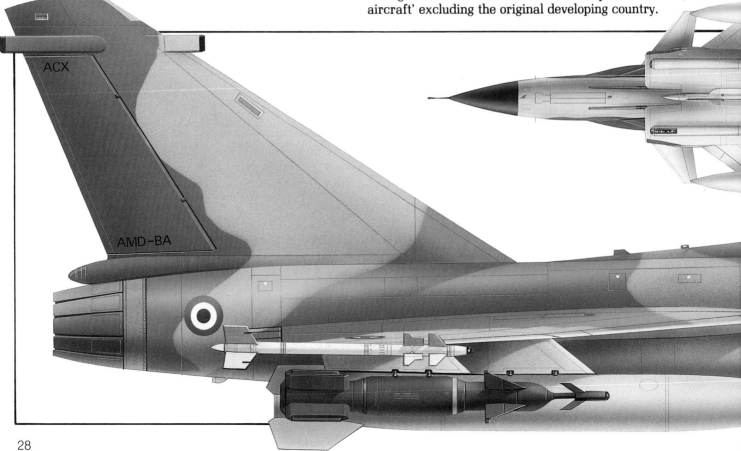

Right: The sole Rafale prototype pulling up into a loop, with Magic missiles on the wingtips. Known as Rafale A, it is slightly larger than the proposed Rafale D and M.

Below: this plan view of a "Rafale D" is highly provisional, nobody quite knowing what it will look like. Weapons depicted are Super 530D AAMs and laser-guided bombs.

Below: A plan view, based on the existing Rafale A prototype. The data in the box opposite refers to the existing prototype. Dassault-Breguet hopes to make the production version smaller and lighter.

Left: Side elevation of the Rafale A prototype, but incorporating features expected to be in the production version.

Eurofighter EFA

In 1982 the British Ministry of Defence and British industry jointly funded a single demonstrator, the EAP (Experimental Aircraft Programme).

This EAP is a valuable research tool, as close as possible to the Eurofighter. Its engines are RB.199 Mk 104D turbofans. The structure is a mix of advanced light alloys, superplastic-formed titanium, glassfibre, carbon fibre (for almost the entire basic wings and foreplanes) and some other composites. Control surfaces comprise the foreplanes, flaperons, leading-edge droops and rudder. The ventral engine inlet has a hinged lower lip ('varicowl'). Speedbrakes are hinged above the rear fuselage.

The Eurofighter EFA will probably have several stores attachments under each wing, and electronic-warfare pods on the tips. Its radar will fit into a slightly slimmer nose, and the vertical tail will probably be smaller and simpler.

Eurofighter EFA GmbH has been formed by British Aerospace (right wing, front fuselage and canard, 33%), MBB of West Germany (centre fuselage and fin, 33%, with Dornier as co-partner), Aeritalia (left wing and rear fuselage, 21%) and CASA of Spain (share of right wing and rear fuselage, 13%). The new engines will be produced by the Eurojet consortium owned by Rolls-Royce, MTU, Fiat and Sener of Spain.

Full development of the EuroFighter began in 1988. Eight prototypes will be built, meeting the requirements of the four nations whose air forces will initially require about 800 aircraft. These will be assembled in all four countries, at Warton, Manching, Turin and Madrid.

Origin: European consortium.
Engines: Two Eurojet EJ.200 each in 20,230lb (9,177kg) class.
Dimensions: Not finalized; (EAP) Span 38ft 7½in (11.77m); length 57ft 6¼in (17.53m); height 18ft 1¼in (5.52m); wing area 520ft² (48.3m²). EuroFighter wing area is to be 538ft² (50m²).
Weights: Empty 21,495lb (9,750kg); max about 40,000lb (18,144kg).
Performance: Max speed (with weapons, at high altitude) over 1,320mph (2,135km/h, Mach 2 +); ceiling about 60,000ft (18,288m).
Armament: Provision for a gun; in air-combat role, typically four AIM-120A and two AIM-132 missiles.
History: First flight of EAP demonstrator 8 August 1986.

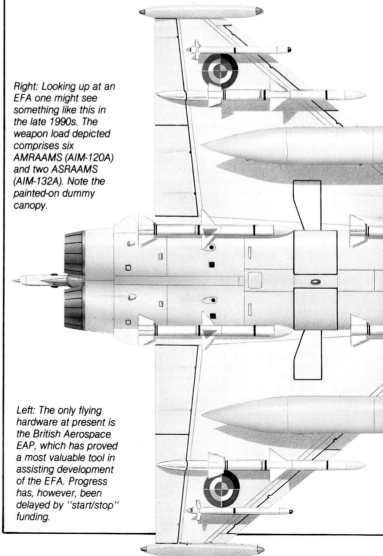

Right: Looking up at an EFA one might see something like this in the late 1990s. The weapon load depicted comprises six AMRAAMS (AIM-120A) and two ASRAAMS (AIM-132A). Note the painted-on dummy canopy.

Left: The only flying hardware at present is the British Aerospace EAP, which has proved a most valuable tool in assisting development of the EFA. Progress has, however, been delayed by "start/stop" funding.

Below: Seen from above EFA might resemble this. Like the rival French Rafale, the EFA is expected to be smaller and lighter than the EAP.

Left: Unusual head-on view of the EAP at the 1987 Paris airshow, with its canard foreplanes at full deflection and leading-edge slats open.

General Dynamics F-16 Fighting Falcon

Starting as a small technology demonstrator, the F-16 matured into a capable multirole fighter. Features include a wing with automatic variable camber from hinged leading and trailing edges, slab horizontal tail, engine fed by a plain ventral inlet modern cockpit with a reclining seat, sidestick force-transducer controller linked to FBW flight controls and an overall concept of relaxed static stability. At the time of its design the F-16's ability to sustain 9g in prolonged turns was unique.

It was in January 1975 that the F-16 was selected as a major type for the USAF inventory, with the total procurement set at 3,047 of the A, B, C and D versions, the B and D being two-seaters, with full avionics and weapons but with 17 per cent less fuel.

In June 1975 the F-16 was selected for Belgium, Denmark, the Netherlands and Norway, mainly to replace the F-104. These countries formed a multinational manufacturing programme.

The FAB (Belgian Air Force) has 116 aircraft, with a follow-on order for 44. Egypt has 120, equipping brigades at Inchas, Al Mansurah and Abu Hammad. Israel has 150 F-16A/B, eight of which, each with two 2,000lb (907kg) bombs, flew a long mission at low level in June 1981 to destroy the Iraqi reactor at Osirak with pinpoint accuracy. Israeli F-16s have seen a lot of action against Syrian MiG-23 'Floggers'.

South Korea received 36. The Netherlands received 102, followed by batches of 22, 18, 12 and 57. Norway bought 72, and Denmark 58 plus 12. Pakistan received 40, and wants a further 60. Other customers include Signapore, Venezuela, Thailand and Indonesia.

Since 1981 USAF F-16s have wiring and system architecture for later updating with LANTIRN night and attack pods, one on each side of the inlet duct, the ASPJ (airborne self-protection jammer) EW system, the APG-68 radar, a giant GEC Avionics wide-angle head-up cockpit display, and the AIM-120A AMRAAM. The upgraded aircraft is the F-16C, the F-16D being the two-seat version.

Since 1985 the F110 engine has been a customer option. The resulting superior aircraft are still designated F-16C and D. About half the USAF aircraft have the F110 engine. So do 60 (or 90) for Israel, 12 for Bahrein, 160 for Turkey, 40 for Greece and 26 F-16N adversary aircraft for the US Navy. The Agile Falcon and a reconnaissance version are being developed.

Above: Condensation makes the writhing wing-root vortices visible in manoeuvres.

Right: Head-on view of an Israeli F-16A with jammer, tanks and rockets.

Origin: United States.
Engine: (A,B) One Pratt & Whitney F100-200 rated at 23,840lb (10,814kg), (C,D) 23,450lb (10,637kg) F100-220, or 27,600lb (12,519kg) General Electric F110-100.
Dimensions: Span (no AAMs) 31ft (9.45m); length 49ft 3in (15.01m); height 16ft 8½in (5.09m); wing area 300ft² (27.87m²).
Weights: Empty (A) 16,234lb (7,364kg), (C) 16,794lb (7,618kg), (D) 17,408lb (7,896kg); max loaded (A,B) 35,400lb (16,057kg), (C,D) 37,500lb (17,010kg).
Performance: Max speed 1,350mph (2,173km/h, Mach 2.05) at 40,000ft (12,190m), (sea level) 910mph (1,470km/h, Mach 1.2); initial climb 50,000ft (15,240m)/min; service ceiling, over 50,000ft (15,240m); tactical radius (A, six Mk 82, internal fuel, hi-lo-hi) 340 miles (547km).
Armament: One M61A-1 20mm gun with 500/515 rounds; seven pylons for max load 11,950lb (5,420kg) for 9g.
History: First flight (YF-16) 20 January 1974, (F-16A) 7 August 1978.

Left: Plan view of an F-16A showing Sparrow AAMs, which were launched (but not guided) in the early test programme. On the centreline is an ALQ-131 ECM jammer pod.

Above: F-16A of the US Air Force in Exercise Team Spirit '85.

Above: F-16As through Block 5 had a smaller tailplane (left). The standard tail is graphite/epoxy.

Above: The standard tail (left) can be replaced by an extended box for a drag chute or ECM system.

Above: Side elevation of an early F-16A of the first unit, the USAF 388th TFW at Hill AFB, Utah. It is depicted with AIM-120A

(AMRAAM) missiles on wing pylons; these are to be integrated in an upgrade programme.

Grumman F-14 Tomcat

Origin: United States.
Engines: (F-14A) Two Pratt & Whitney TF30-414A rated at 20,900lb (9,480kg); (A Plus, D) two 27,600lb (12,519kg) General Electric F110-400.
Dimensions: Span (68° sweep) 38ft 2in (11.63m), (20° sweep) 64ft 1½in (19.54m); length 62ft 8in (19.1m); height 16ft (4.88m); wing area (spread) 565ft² (52.49m²).
Weights: Empty 40,104lb (18,191kg); loaded (clean) 58,715lb (26,632kg), (max) 73,349lb (33,724kg).
Performance: Max speed 1,564mph (2,517km/h, Mach 2.34) at altitude, 910mph (1,470km/h, Mach 1.2) at sea level; initial climb over 30,000ft (9,144m)/min; service ceiling over 56,000ft (17,070m); range (external fuel) about 2,000 miles (3,200km).
Armament: One 20mm M61A-1 gun; four AIM-7 Sparrow and four or eight AIM-9 Sidewinder air-to-air missiles, or up to six AIM-54 Phoenix and two AIM-9.
History: First flight 21 December 1970; initial deployment October 1972.

The F-14 has had a long career with virtually no major modification, and will remain in production until the 1990s with updates to the avionics and a new engine. Throughout its career the engine has been the only continual source of worry. The immense range and multiple-target capability of the radar and AAMs carried puts the aircraft in a class of its own.

Features include pilot and naval flight officer in Martin-Baker seats, a retractable refuelling probe, variable inlet ducts, swing wings, full-span slats, flaps and roll-control spoilers (the latter augmented by the horizontal tails), twin vertical tails, and retractable canards called glove vanes.

The AWG-9 radar has a 36in (0.914m) planar antenna and operates in many modes but usually in pulse/doppler to indicate targets out to 195 miles (315km). It can track 24 targets while simultaneously engaging any selected six.

By mid-1988 Grumman had delivered 660 F-14s, almost all of them F-14As. In 1987 production switched to the F110-powered F-14A Plus; two years later it will again

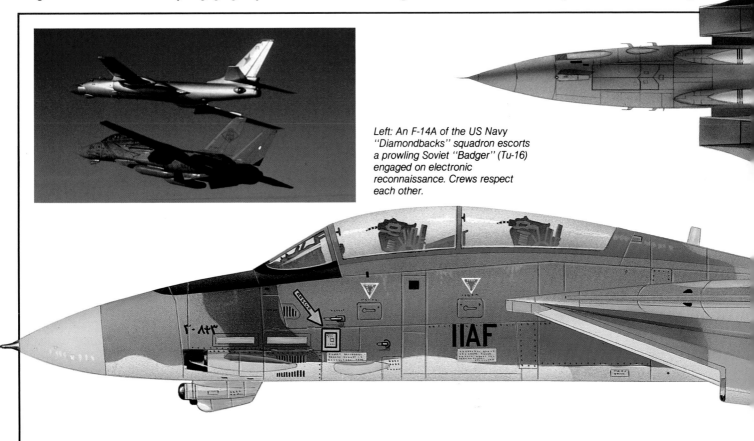

Left: An F-14A of the US Navy "Diamondbacks" squadron escorts a prowling Soviet "Badger" (Tu-16) engaged on electronic reconnaissance. Crews respect each other.

change, to the F-14D, with new digital avionics, new cockpit displays, improved radar, ASPJ, JTIDS and the AIM-120A AMRAAM missile.

Grumman supplied 80 F-14As to Iran, where about half have fought in the war with Iraq. Support from the USA has been withheld.

The rest of the F-14s serve with US Navy VFs 1, 2, 11, 14, 21, 24, 31, 32, 33, 41, 51, 74, 84, 101, 102, 103, 111, 114, 124, 142, 143, 154, 211 and 213. Two aircraft from VF-41 over the Gulf of Sidra on 19 August 1981 were attacked by two Libyan Su-22s, which were destroyed.

The F-14 has an auto wingsweep programmer. Most have a chin FLIR, APN-154 radar beacon and ACLS (Automatic Carrier Landing System) antenna, but since 1982 Northrop has been supplying the TCS (TV Camera Set), showing the crew a wide-angle picture of targets for acquisition, followed by a narrow magnified image for identification, at beyond visual distance. Another optional store is TARPS (Tactical Air Reconnaissance Pod System), with a frame camera, lateral oblique camera and IR linescan.

Below: Plan view of a US Navy F-14A, showing typical "heavy" armament of four AIM-54 Phoenix and four AIM-9 Sidewinder AAMs. Some F-14As are also able to carry TARPS (see text).

Below: Side elevation of an F-14A of the Islamic Iranian AF. As this book went to press an Iranian A300B was shot down 'in mistake for an F-14'!

IAI Kfir, Nesher (Dagger)

The Nesher (Eagle) is a Mirage 5, powered by an Atar 9C but equipped with Israeli avionics. Substantial numbers were sold to Argentina, survivors from the Falklands War being equipped with inflight-refuelling probes, with IAI engineering support.

The Kfir (Lion Cub) is a redesigned aircraft with the J79 engine, enlarged ducts, a new engine bay of reduced length, a new dorsal fin with ram inlet, a revised cockpit, a new nose, a new fuel system, strengthened, longer-stroke main landing gears and avionics of Israeli origin. The first two aircraft were delivered in June 1975.

In the Kfir C2, small strakes along the sides of the nose and removable (but fixed-incidence) foreplanes above the inlets

Origin: Israel.
Engine: (Except Nesher) 17,900lb (8,119kg) General Electric J79-J1E.
Dimensions: (Nesher) As Mirage 5; (Kfir) span 26ft 11½in (8.22m); length (C2) 51ft 4½in (15.65m), (C2 with Elta radar) 53ft 11½in (16.45m), (TC2) 54ft 1in (16.49m); height 14ft 11in (4.55m); wing area 374.6ft² (34.8m²).
Weights: (Kfir) Empty (C2, interceptor) 16,060lb (7,285kg); loaded, (C2, max) 32,340lb (14,670kg).
Performance: (C2) Max speed (clean) 863mph (1,389km/h) at sea level, over 1,516mph (2,440km/h, Mach 2.3) above 36,090ft (11,000m); initial climb 45,950ft (14,000m)/min; service ceiling 58,000ft (17,680m); combat radius, (attack, three tanks plus seven bombs and two Shafrir, hi-lo-hi) 477 miles (768km).
Armament: Two IAI-built DEFA 5-52 guns each with 140 rounds; seven hardpoints for a total of 9,469lb (4,295kg) including two Shafrir 2 AAMs (outer wings) plus tanks, bombs (ten 500lb/227kg), Gabriel III, Maverick or Hobos missiles, rocket pods, Matra Durandal or other anti-runway weapons, napalm, ECM pods and tanks.
History: First flight (Nesher) reportedly September 1969, (Kfir prototype) 1972, (production) 1974, (C2) 1975, (TC2) February 1981, (C7) 1983.

improved low-speed and combat-manoeuvre capability, which was further enhanced by extending the outer wing leading edge with a sharp dogtooth. The C2 has shorter take-off and landing run, a steeper landing approach in a flatter attitude and a reduced gust reponse in low-level attack.

The standard C2 has an extended nose housing the Elta EL/M-2001B ranging radar. Equipment includes inertial navigation, comprehensive flight-control and weapon-delivery systems and a high standard of EW/ECM installa-

tions. Further subsystems are in the rear cockpit of the two-seat TC2 version, first flown in 1981, with a down-sloping extended nose. The two-seater is used for conversion training, and as a dedicated EW aircraft.

In 1983 production switched to the Kfir C7, with an uprated engine, increased internal fuel, a new Hotas cockpit, increased gross weight, a digital computer for stores management, the WDNS 341 navigation and weapon-aiming system and, as an option, the big M-2021 pulse-doppler radar.

IAI has delivered about 250 Kfirs, and offers update kits for users of the Mirage. The US Navy has borrowed 12 of the early Kfir (non-canard) fighters from Israel, with contract support by IAI, to try them out as 'hostile' opponents at NAS Oceana. Designated F-21A, they will be replaced by F-16Ns, but meanwhile a further 13 F-21As are being procured for use by the Marines at MCAS Yuma.

Above: Following lease of 12 F-21As (US designation) by the US Navy, this was the first of a follow-on batch of 13 for the Marine Corps.

Left: Looking up at the Kfir-C2, clarifying the slim nose strakes and the triplets of bombs under the fuselage.

Above: This Kfir-C2 was later upgraded to C7 standard, but with few external changes. Weapons are Shafrirs, LAU-10 rocket launchers and Mk 82 bombs.

Lockheed F-104 Starfighter

Designed as a pure air-combat fighter for USAF Tactical Air Command, the F-104 proved to have all the performance needed, but to be disappointing in agility, range and weapons. The programme was rescued by Lockheed's development of the F-104G, with a strengthened airframe and new avionics, with the first inertial navigation system to enter service in a fighter, Nasarr multimode radar, manoeuvring flaps and many other new items. This was selected as its chief new combat type of the Federal German Luftwaffe and Marineflieger.

A total of 1,266 were built in many sub-types including two-seaters used for training and EW missions. Most have been replaced in their original air forces, the main recipient of retired examples being Turkey, who had already purchased 40 new F-104S from Italy. The F-104S was the final variant developed by Lockheed and Aeritalia as an all-

Origin: United States.
Engine: One General Electric J79 turbojet with afterburner; (G RF/RTF, CF) 15,800lb (7,167kg) J79-11A; (S) 17,900lb (8,120kg) J79-19 or J1Q.
Dimensions: Span (without tip tanks) 21ft 22in (6.68m); length 55ft 9in (16.69m); height 13ft 6in (4.11m); wing area 196.1sq ft (18.22m²).
Weights: Empty 14,082lb (6,387kg), (F-104S, 14,900lb, 6,760kg); max 28,779lb (13,054kg), (F-104S, 31,000lb, 14,060kg).
Performance: Max speed 1,450mph (2,334km/h, Mach 2.2); initial climb 50,000ft (15,250m)/min; service ceiling 58,000ft (17,680m) (zoom ceiling over 90,000ft, 27,400m) range with max weapons about 300 miles (483km), range with four drop tanks (high altitude, subsonic) 1,815 miles (2,920km).
Armament: In most versions, centreline rack rated at 2,000lb (907kg) and two underwing pylons each rated at 1,000lb (454kg) additional racks for small missiles (eg Sidewinder) on fuselage, under wings or on tips; certain versions have reduced fuel and one 20mm M61 Vulcan multi-barrel gun in fuselage; (S) M61 gun, two Sparrow or Aspide and two Sidewinder.
History: First flight (XF-104) 7 February 1954; (F-104A) 17 February 1956; (F-104G) 5 October 1960; (F-104S) 30 December 1968; final delivery from Aeritalia (F-104S) 1975.

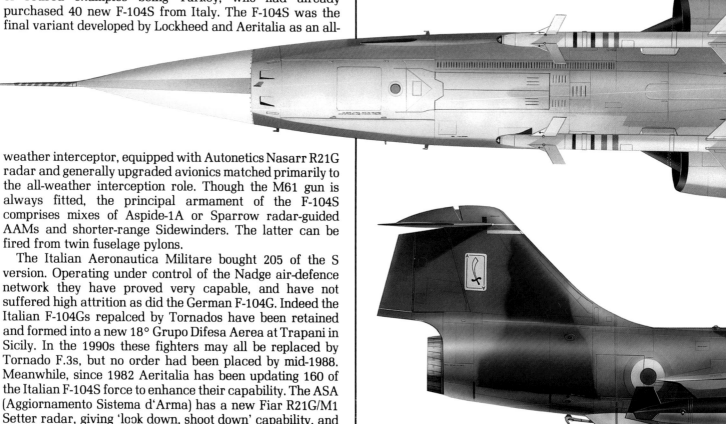

weather interceptor, equipped with Autonetics Nasarr R21G radar and generally upgraded avionics matched primarily to the all-weather interception role. Though the M61 gun is always fitted, the principal armament of the F-104S comprises mixes of Aspide-1A or Sparrow radar-guided AAMs and shorter-range Sidewinders. The latter can be fired from twin fuselage pylons.

The Italian Aeronautica Militare bought 205 of the S version. Operating under control of the Nadge air-defence network they have proved very capable, and have not suffered high attrition as did the German F-104G. Indeed the Italian F-104Gs repalced by Tornados have been retained and formed into a new 18° Grupo Difesa Aerea at Trapani in Sicily. In the 1990s these fighters may all be replaced by Tornado F.3s, but no order had been placed by mid-1988. Meanwhile, since 1982 Aeritalia has been updating 160 of the Italian F-104S force to enhance their capability. The ASA (Aggiornamento Sistema d'Arma) has a new Fiar R21G/M1 Setter radar, giving 'look down, shoot down' capability, and many other avionics upgrades. Deliveries of the improved ASA aircraft have been in progress since November 1986.

Above: These F-104S Starfighters
serve with the Italian AF's 6° wing
at Ghedi (Brescia) in the
fighter/attack roles.

Above: Plan view of an ASA
upgraded Starfighter, showing
285gal (1,287 lit) tip tanks, twin
Aspide AAMs and four close-range
AIM-9J Sidewinders.

Below: Side elevation of the same
aircraft, showing markings of the
53° Stormo (wing) based at Cameri.
The big radar-guided Aspide is a
great asset.

McDonnell Douglas F-4 Phantom II

By far the most important fighter in the non-Communist world during the past 30 years, the F-4 has an evergreen quality of sheer capability. Altogether 5,195 were built.

The F-4A and F-4B for the US Navy introduced blown flaps and drooped leading edges, radar-guided Sparrow AAMs pylons for tanks, Sidewinders, bombs or other stores, tremendous internal fuel capacity, tandem seats for pilot and RIO (radar intercept officer) and a powerful radar. This family continued via the F-4J to today's F-4N and F-4S rebuilds with more fuel, revised structure and avionics, slatted wings and tailplanes, and other updates.

The USAF F-4C of 1963 proved so satisfactory that the Air Force was allowed to have its own F-4D, with ground attack avionics. This was followed by the F-4E with uprated engines, an extra tank, new radar, M61 gun and, in the course of production, powerful slats instead of the blown droops.

West Germany chose a simpler F-4F without Sparrow AAMs. Mitsubishi assembled 138 F-4E(J) in Japan. Britain bought the F-4K (Phantom FG.1) for the Navy and F-4M (FGR.2) for the RAF, with Spey engines, INS, AWG-11/12 radar fire control, strike camera and fin-cap RWR.

Tornados are replacing RAF Phantoms, but to replace Falklands aircraft 15 ex-USN fighters form No 74 Sqn where they are known as F-4J(UK).

The USAF contracted for the RF-4C, which set a new standard in multisensor reconnaissance without armament. The Marines bought RF-4Bs with similar equipment the RF-4E is based on the F-4E.

The F-4G Advanced Wild Weasel carries the APR-38 EW system whose 52 special aerials include large pods facing forwards under the nose and to the rear above the rudder. The system is governed by a Texas Instruments computer with reprogrammable software to keep up to date on all known hostile emitters. The aircraft carries such weapons as triplets of the AGM-65 EO-guided Maverick precision attack weapon, Shrike ARM (anti-radar missile) and HARM (high-speed ARM).

In 1986 Germany's F-4Fs and Japan's F-4E (J)s were the subjects of major update programmes to fit look-down pulse-doppler radars. Meanwhile, Boeing and Pratt & Whitney have tried to re-engine F-4s with the PW1120, one being converted at IAI in Israel.

Origin: United States.
Engines: (C,D,RF) Two 17,000lb (7,711kg) General Electric J79-15 turbojets; (E,F,G) 17,900lb (8,120kg) J79-17; (J,N,S) 17,900lb J79-10; (K,M) 20,515lb (9,305kg) Rolls-Royce Spey 202/203.
Dimensions: Span 38ft 5in (11.7m); length (C,D,J,N,S) 58ft 3in (17.76m), (E,G,F and all RF versions) 62ft 11in or 63ft (19.2m), (K,M) 57ft 7in (17.55m); height (all) 16ft 3in (4.96m); wing area 530ft² (49.2m²).
Weights: Empty (C,D,J,N) 28,000lb (12,700kg), (E,F, RF) 29,000lb (13,150kg), (G,K,M) 31,000lb (14,060kg); max (C,D,J,K,M,N,RF) 58,000lb (26,308kg), (E,G,F) 60,630lb (27,502kg).
Performance: Max speed with Sparrow missiles only (lo) 910mph (1,470km/h, Mach 1.2) with J79 engines, 920mph with Spey, (hi) 1,500mph (2,414km/h, Mach 2.27) with J79, 1,386mph with Spey; service ceiling 60,000ft (19,685m); range (internal fuel) about 1,750 miles (2,817km).
Armament: (All versions except RF models which have no armament) Four AIM-7 Sparrow or Sky Flash (later AMRAAM) air-to-air missiles recessed under fuselage; inner wing pylons can carry two more AIM-7 or four AIM-9 Sidewinder missiles; E versions except RF also have internal 20mm M61 gun, and five pylons for stores to 16,000lb (7,257kg).
History: First flight (XF4H-1) 27 May 1958; delivery February 1961.

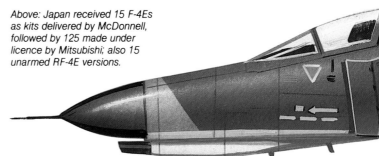

Above: Japan received 15 F-4Es as kits delivered by McDonnell, followed by 125 made under licence by Mitsubishi; also 15 unarmed RF-4E versions.

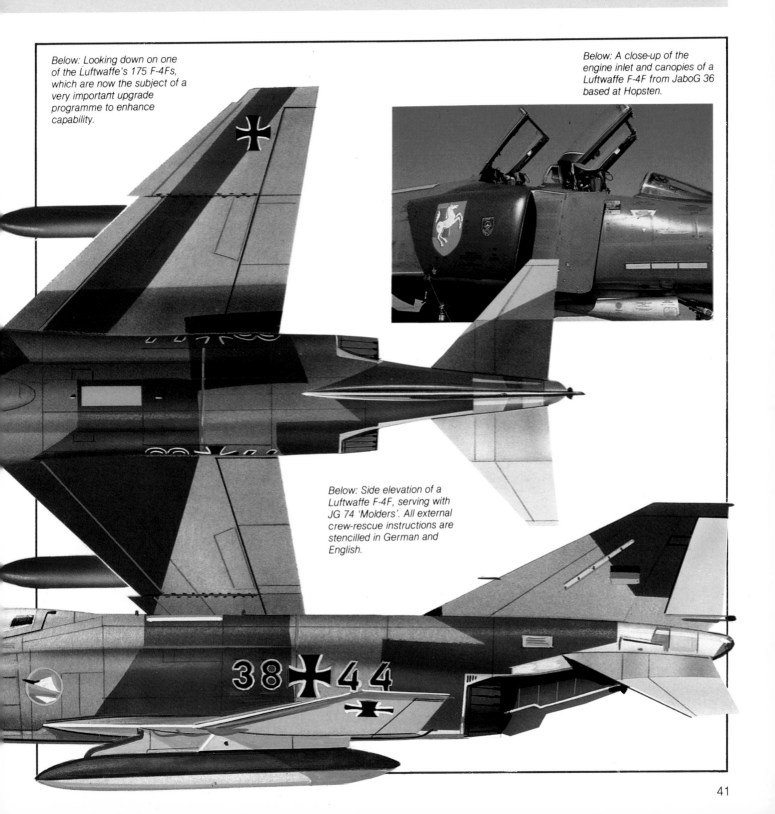

Below: Looking down on one of the Luftwaffe's 175 F-4Fs, which are now the subject of a very important upgrade programme to enhance capability.

Below: A close-up of the engine inlet and canopies of a Luftwaffe F-4F from JaboG 36 based at Hopsten.

Below: Side elevation of a Luftwaffe F-4F, serving with JG 74 'Molders'. All external crew-rescue instructions are stencilled in German and English.

McDonnell Douglas F-15 Eagle

Origin: United States.
Engines: Two Pratt & Whitney F100-100 rated at 23,930lb (10,855kg); (E) two 23,450lb (10,640kg) F100-220.
Dimensions: Span 42ft 9¾in (13.05m); length 63ft 9in (19.43m); height 18ft 5½in (5.63m); wing area 608ft² (56.5m²).
Weights: Empty (A) 27,381lb (12,420kg); take-off (intercept mission, A) 42,206lb (19,145kg); max (A) 56,000lb (25,401kg), (C,FAST packs) 68,000lb (30,845kg), (E) 81,000lb (36,742kg).
Performance: Max speed (clean, over 45,000ft/13,716m) 1,650mph (2,655km/h, Mach 2.5), (clean, sea level) 910mph (1,470km/h, Mach 1.2); combat ceiling (A, clean) 63,000ft (19,200m).
Armament: One 20mm M61A1 gun with 940 rounds; four AIM-7 or eight AIM-120A, plus four AIM-9; plus bomb capability.
History: First flight 27 July 1972; delivery (inventory) November 1974.

Most observers in the Western World regard the F-15 as the natural successor to the F-4, as the best fighter in the world. To a considerable degree its qualities rest on the giant fixed-geometry wing, F100 engine and Hughes APG-63 pulse-doppler radar.

The lower edge of the fuselage is tailored to the medium-range AAMs. The gun is at the root of the right wing, drawing ammunition from a tank inboard of the duct. Roll is by ailerons at low speeds, the dogtoothed slab tailplanes taking over at above Mach 1.

Avionics include a pulse-doppler radar, vertical situation display, HUD, INS and a digital computer. In its integral ECM/IFF subsystems the F-15 is better than most Western fighters, with radar warning internal countermeasures, EW warning set and IFF with reply-evaluator. High-power jammers must still be hung externally.

USAF orders total 1,266, plus 51 for Israel, 62 for Saudi Arabia and 187 for Japan (173 assembled in Japan). Current production is centred on the F-15C and two-seat F-15D, with programmable signal processor increase in memory capacity, extra internal fuel and conformal pallets, called FAST (Fuel and Sensor, Tactical) packs to add 9,750lb (4,422kg) fuel.

In 1983 tangential carriage was introduced, enabling 12 bombs of 1,000lb (454kg) to be hung on stub pylons along the lower edges of the FAST packs, giving reduced drag and leaving the existing pylons free. The F-15E is configured equally for the surface attack and air superiority roles. A tandem-seater, it has APG-70 high-resolution radar, with DBS (doppler beam sharpening), new computer, a wide-field HUD, an internal ASPJ ECM, LANTIRN all-weather nav/targeting pods, and multifunction displays for managing the mission.

McDonnell is modifying an F-15 with canard foreplanes, part-vectoring engine nozzles and other changes. It is intended to have enhanced manoeuvrability and to operate from runways 'shorter than 1,500ft (457m)'.

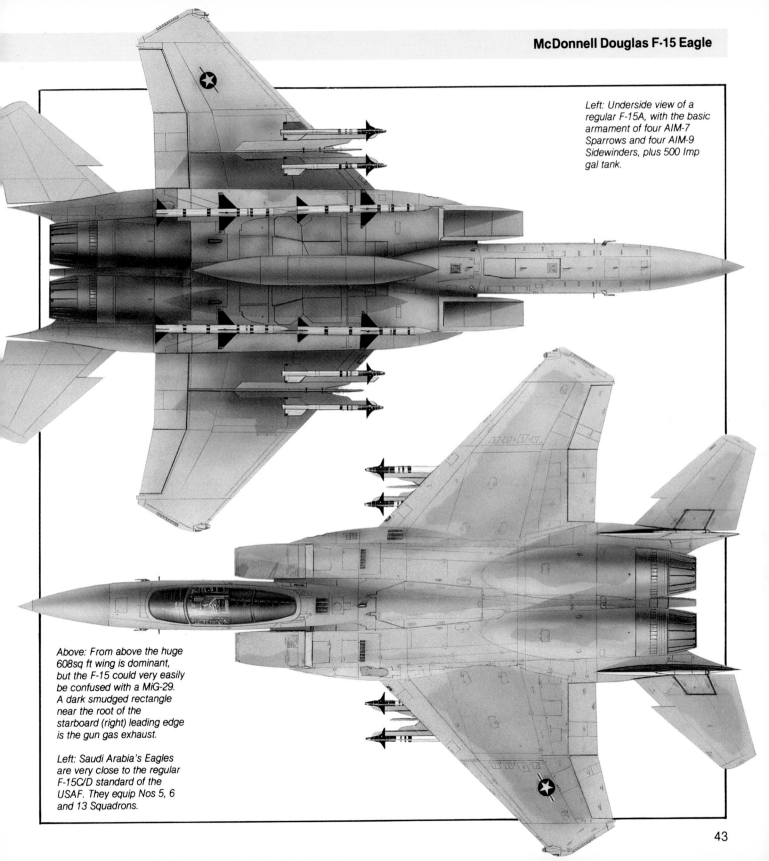

Left: Underside view of a regular F-15A, with the basic armament of four AIM-7 Sparrows and four AIM-9 Sidewinders, plus 500 Imp gal tank.

Above: From above the huge 608sq ft wing is dominant, but the F-15 could very easily be confused with a MiG-29. A dark smudged rectangle near the root of the starboard (right) leading edge is the gun gas exhaust.

Left: Saudi Arabia's Eagles are very close to the regular F-15C/D standard of the USAF. They equip Nos 5, 6 and 13 Squadrons.

McDonnell Douglas F/A-18 Hornet

From the outset in 1974 the Hornet was designed to be equally good in both fighter and attack roles, replacing the F-4 in the first and the A-7 in the second. Unlike its rival, the F-16, it has from the start carried a high-power radar matched with radar-guided AAMs. In the long-range interdiction role shortcomings centre on radius with a given weapon load, though this can be rectified by using larger external tanks and air refuelling.

The cockpit is a major 'plus', with Hotas controls (the stick being conventional instead of a sidestick), up-front CNI controls and three MFDs (multifunction displays) which replace traditional instruments. This is not to deny that a second crew member would ease the workload.

There is a dual-pilot version for conversion training; this retains the weapons capability and radar, but has 6 per cent less internal fuel. There is also a prototype of a dedicated reconnaissance F/A-18(R), testing of which began in August 1984, while the US Marines are to use the two-seat RF-18D with a multisensor pod.

The first Navy/Marines training squadron, VFA-125, commissioned at NAS Lemoore in November 1980. By spring 1988 the Navy/Marines had equipped 27 squadrons with 460 aircraft. Current F/A-18Cs and two-seat Ds have a major upgrade in avionics, with night attack capability from October 1989.

In 1984 a structural problem surfaced — cracking of the tips of the fins and the fin/fuselage attachment. As an interim measure, the angle of attack was limited to 25° below 30,000ft when the aircraft was flying at between 300 and 400kts. Modification kits were installed in the field, while modified fins entered production later that year.

The Canadian CF-188 differs in small items such as having a spotlight for the visual identification of aircraft at night. Canada has only a small manufacturing offset (Canadair makes nose sections), despite the size of the order — 138 aircraft, including 24 TF-18s. Deliveries took place in 1982-88.

Australia's buy of 57, plus 18 TFs, triggered a complex involvement of local industry. The first two TFs were delivered from St Louis in May 1985, and the rest are being assembled by ATA with Australian content. Spain bought 72 (plus 12 options) EF-18s. South Korea was the main sales target in 1988, and various Super Hornets have been proposed for Europe and Japan. Predictably, these feature uprated F404 engines, canard foreplanes, a "cranked arrow" wing, new tail surfaces and more composite structure.

Origin: United States.
Engines: Two General Electric F404-400 each rated at 16,000lb (7,258kg).
Dimensions: Span (with missiles) 40ft 4¾in (12.31m); length 56ft (17.07m); height 15ft 3½in (4.66m); wing area 400ft² (36.16m²).
Weights: Empty 23,050lb (10,455kg); loaded (fighter) 36,710lb (16,651kg), (attack) 49,224lb (22,328kg).
Performance: Max speed (clean, at altitude) 1,190mph (1,915km/h, Mach 1.8) ceiling 49,000ft (14,935m); combat radius (fighter) 461 miles (741km).
Armament: One 20mm M61 gun with 570 rounds; nine weapon stations for max load (catapult) of 13,400lb (6,080kg) or (land) 17,000lb (7,711kg).
History: First flight (YF-17) 9 June 1974, (first of 11 test F-18s) 18 November 1978, (production F/A-18) 1980; service entry 1982.

Right: Looking up at an F/A-18A armed with AIM-9L Sidewinders, AIM-7M Sparrows, Mk 83 GP bombs and three 275gal (1,250lit) drop tanks.

Below: Side view of the same aircraft, serving with VFA-125 Rough Riders, the Pacific Fleet Readiness (training) squadron based at NAS Lemoore.

Above: Flares released by aircraft of Marine squadron VMFA-531 Gray Ghosts, based at MCAS El Toro, California, when not carrier-embarked.

Below: Northrop failed to get a launch customer for the far superior land-based F-18L, whose right wing is seen here (no fold, flaperons).

MiG-21, J-7 (Fishbed, Mongol)

Several thousand MiG-21s of many versions remain in service with 38 air forces. All are small tailed-delta fighters with a generally rather limited capability.

Most aircraft by late 1961 had a side-hinged canopy with fixed screen and blown flaps which reduced the field length. By 1965 the PFS and PFM had introduced the F2S-300 engine, R2L radar and gunpack. The MiG-21PFMA has 'Jay Bird' radar, four pylons and an enlarged dorsal spine.

Up to this point all models had dual trainer versions (NATO name 'Mongol'), though most MiG-21U trainers are based on early series, including the Chinese Guizhou JJ-7 (FT-7). Chinese production has been of early 66-series 21Fs, though the upgraded F-7M Airguard is available for export.

By 1968 Soviet production featured 20 fits of EW equipment, cameras and flash cartridges, some being 21R and RF reconnaissance versions with SLAR. Main models are the MF fighter-bomber, the SMB with a giant dorsal tank spine, and the MiG-21bis with the R-25 engine and further improved avionics.

The latest version is the Sabre II, proposed by Grumman for Pakistan, based on the F-7M but with a large radar and side inlets feeding a new US turbofan engine.

Below: Plan view of a MiG-21SMT, the variant with the greatest capacity in the dorsal spine (but not the highest flight performance).

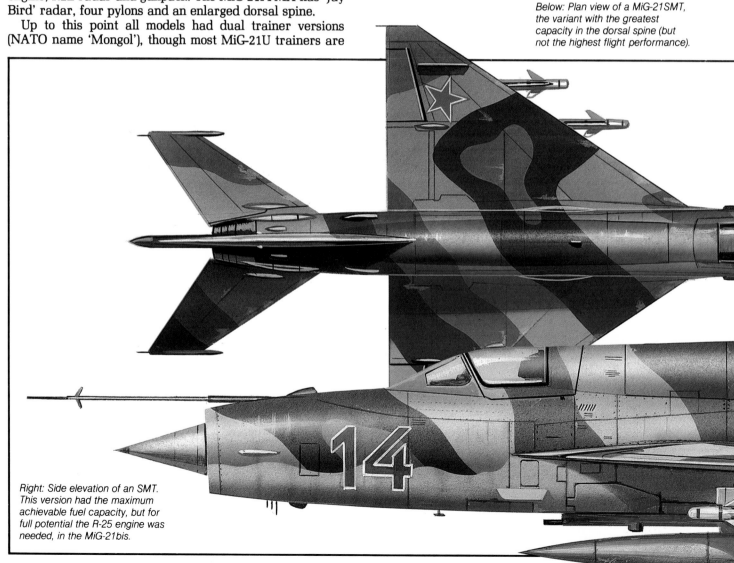

Right: Side elevation of an SMT. This version had the maximum achievable fuel capacity, but for full potential the R-25 engine was needed, in the MiG-21bis.

Origin: Soviet Union.
Engine: (MF,RF,SMT,UM, early 21bis) 14,550lb (6,600kg) Tumanskii R-13-300, (21bis) 16,535lb (7,500kg) R-25.
Dimensions: Span 23ft 5½in (7.15m); length (including boom) 51ft 8½in (15.76m); height (typical) 13ft 5½in (4.1m); wing area 247.57ft² (23m²).
Weights: Empty, (MF) about 12,300lb (5,580kg), (bis) 12,600lb (5,715kg); loaded (typical, half internal fuel and two K-13A) 15,000lb (6,800kg); max (bis, two K-13A and three drop tanks) 23,148lb (10,500kg).
Performance: Max speed (typical, sea level) 800mph (1,290km/h, Mach 1.05), (36,000ft/11,000m, clean) 1,385mph (2,230km/h, Mach 2.1); initial climb, (bis) 58,000ft (17,680m)/min; practical ceiling (all) rarely above 50,000ft (15,240m); range with internal fuel (bis) 683 miles (1,100km).
Armament: (FL and subsequent) one GSh-23L gun with 200 rounds, and four pylons for up to 3,307lb (1,500kg). HAL-built aircraft carry Magic AAMs, J-7s CAA-1 and -2 AAMs.
History: First flight (Ye-50) November 1955, service delivery (21) 1959.

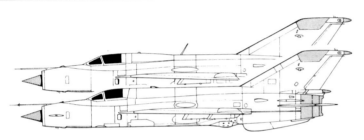

Left: Among the numerous versions of this famous aircraft were the PFM (rear) with the new windscreen and canopy, and the MF (foreground) with many changes.

Above: Production at Hindustan Aerospace at Nasik, India, showing MiG-21bis in final assembly. Later the MiG-27M was built; the MiG-29 may follow.

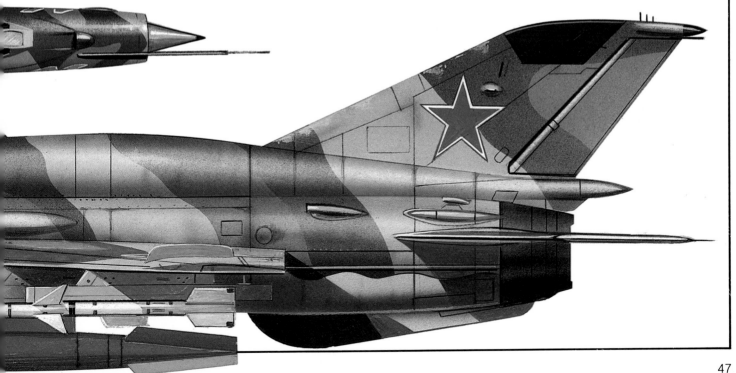

MiG-23 ('Flogger')

Built at a higher rate than any other combat aircraft the past ten years, the MiG-23 has the same aerodynamics as the Su-24, but is smaller and half as powerful. The VG wing gives great lift for take-off and loiter with heavy loads of fuel and weapons, and in the MiG-23MF interceptor roughly doubles patrol endurance to almost 4hr. With the wings at 72° the aircraft is ideally configured for interception with stand-off missiles or for attack on a surface target.

All versions have more or less the same airframe, designed to a load factor of 8g and for operation from rough airstrips. The first production series was the MiG-23MF, in various sub-types called 'Flogger-B' by NATO. This usually carries the J-band radar called 'High Lark', IFF, ILS and IR sensor. Sirena 3 radar warning is fitted, with ECM threat-analysis and jamming, though for penetrating high-threat areas jammer/flare/chaff dispensers must occupy at least one pylon. The radar has significant capability against low-level targets

Origin: Soviet Union.
Engine: (Most) One Tumanskii R-29 rated at 27,560lb (12,500kg), (S, SM and U) 22,485lb (10,200kg) R-27.
Dimensions: Span (72° sweep) 26ft 9⅔in (8.17m), (16°) 46ft 9in (14.25m); length (most, exc probe) 55ft 1½in (16.8m); height 14ft 4in (4.35m); wing area (16°) 293.4ft² (27.26m²).
Weights: Empty (MF) 24,250lb (11,000kg); loaded (clean, MF) 34,390lb (15,600kg); max (BM, two tanks and six FAB-500) 44,312lb (20,100kg).
Performance: Max speed (hi, clean MF) 1,553mph (2,500km/h, Mach 2.35), (sea level) 910mph (1,470km/h, Mach 1.2); ceiling (MF) 61,000ft (18,600m); combat radius (MF, fighter mission) 560–805 miles.
Armament: (23MF interceptor) One 23mm GSh-23L gun with 200 rounds, two R-23R (AA-7 'Apex') and four R-60 (AA-8 'Aphid') AAMs.
History: First flight (Ye-231) probably 1966; service entry (23S) 1971.

and the MF has demonstrated ability to engage targets at far above its own altitude using the large R-23R missile.

The trainer version has a slimmer nose housing R2L radar, two stepped cockpits with separate hinged canopies, a periscope for the instructor at the rear and a larger dorsal spine covering the larger air-conditioning system.

A variant of the MF, called 'Flogger-G', has a smaller dorsal fin and has been seen with a new undernose sensor pod.

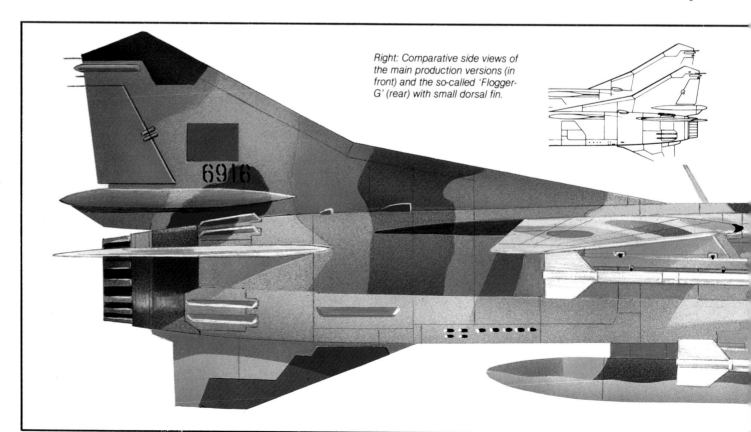

Right: Comparative side views of the main production versions (in front) and the so-called 'Flogger-G' (rear) with small dorsal fin.

Above: A recent (1987?) picture of a 'Flogger-G' with wings at minimum sweep and R-23R (Apex) missiles on the glove pylons.

Below: Plan view of a typical MiG-23 all-weather interceptor, with wings at an intermediate angle. Like many Soviet aircraft, its performance was under-rated until1988, when the full potential was reluctantly admitted.

Above: Side elevation of an early production MiG-23MF 'Flogger-E' of the Libyan Arab AF. The AAMs are of the K-13A (AA-2 'Atoll') sub-type.

MiG-25 (Foxbat)

The fastest combat aircraft ever put into service, the MiG-25 was originally designed to intercept the USAF RS-70 Valkyrie (which was cancelled). Speed and agility being incompatible, the MiG-25 is a 'straight line' aircraft. It takes time to work up to full speed, burning fuel at a prodigious rate, and once at Mach 2.8 (the limit with AAMs) the aircraft has a turn radius of many miles.

The wing is tapered on the leading edge and set at 4° anhedral. The slim fuselage merges into giant flanking air ducts with doors above and below, large bleed outlets, a variable roof profile and variable transverse control shutters. About 3,850gal (17,500l) of special T-6 fuel is housed in nine welded-steel tanks. The basic airframe material is steel, with leading edges of titanium.

The only movable surfaces comprise powered ailerons well inboard, powered slab tailplanes, twin powered rudders and plain flaps (apparently not blown). Twin ventral fins incorporate tail bumpers, with an airbrake between them, and twin braking parachutes can be streamed from the rear of the dorsal spine.

The original radar, called 'Fox Fire' by NATO, was a typical 1959 set, of great size and weight and using vacuum tubes. Its rated output of 600kW was used to burn through hostile jamming, but even the earliest MiG-25 interceptors were well equipped with EW systems. CW illuminating transmitters occupy the front of each wing-tip fairing in this version.

Apart from the uprated engne, the 25M ('Foxbat-E') has a completely new radar and many other avionics improvements, though full details are not yet known. The airframe is still severely limited at low altitudes (according to one report, to Mach 0.8), but the 25M is said to have a low-level interception capability 'somewhat comparable to Flogger'. The only visible distinguishing feature of the 25M is an undernose sensor similar to the IR fairing carried by the 23MF. The MiG-31 Foxhound is described separately.

Compared with the MiG-25 interceptor, the reconnaissance versions have a wing of reduced area, with slightly less span and constant sweep from root to tip. The nose radar is removed, giving a conical nose offering reduced drag; inside this (in the basic version known to NATO as 'Foxbat-B) are five large vertical, forward oblique, lateral and panoramic cameras and a SLAR 'looking' through a dielectric panel on the left side of the nose. Doppler radar is believed to be fitted, as on many of the interceptor version. 'Foxbat-D' is a less common variant with a much larger SLAR installation and probably IR linescan but no cameras. About 160 MiG-25Rs of both models are estimated to be in Soviet service, plus about 45 with foreign customers, including eight with No 106 Sqn, Indian AF.

The MiG-25U trainer has the instructor cockpit in front of and below the original cockpit (occupied by the pupil), which is not only the reverse of normal procedure but means that the extra cockpit displaces the radar not fuel.

Below left: Few fighter pilots have got this close! The MiG-25 is a Libyan 'Foxbat-A' with just two huge AA-6 'Acrid' missiles.

Below: One of the first good photographs to show the MiG-25M 'Foxbat-E'. Note the four AA-6 missiles (two radar guided and two infra-red).

Origin: Soviet Union.
Engines: (Most) Two Tumanskii R-31 each rated at 27,120lb (12,300kg), (M) two 30,865lb (14,000kg) R-31F.
Dimensions: Span 45ft 9in (13.95m), (25R) 44ft (13.4m); length 73ft 2in (22.3m); height 18ft 4½in (5.6m); wing area 611.7ft² (56.83m²), (25R) 603ft² (56m²).
Weights: (Typical) Empty equipped (25) just over 44,090lb (20,000kg); max loaded (25) 79,800lb (36,200kg).
Performance: Max speed (36,000ft/11,000m and above, 4 AAMs) 1,850mph (2,987km/h, Mach 2.8); max climb rate 40,950ft (12,480m)/min; service ceiling (25) 80,000ft (24,400m), radius 710 miles.
Armament: Four wing pylons for AA-6 'Acrid' AAM (usually two radar, two IR); or combinations of AA-6, R-23R and R-60.
History: First flight (Ye-26) 1964, (MiG-25) 1969; delivery 1970.

Above left: This head-on view, like the drawing below, shows IR missiles on the inboard pylons and radar-homing AA-6s outboard.

Above: A near-vertical view of the unarmed 'Foxbat-B' at left and the 'Foxbat-D'. Note their needle-like noses, without the fighter's radar.

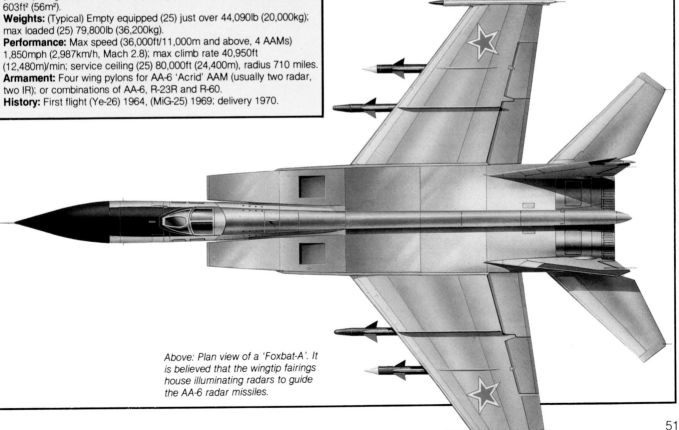

Above: Plan view of a 'Foxbat-A'. It is believed that the wingtip fairings house illuminating radars to guide the AA-6 radar missiles.

MiG-29 (Fulcrum)

From the start it was evident the MiG-29 closely resembles the bigger Su-27, showing that a TsAGI (Central Aero and Hydrodynamics Institute) 'best configuration' has been built by the two OKBs but in different sizes. The Soviet fighters have a low-mounted wing, though this is obscured by the engines added beneath. The inlets are automatically shut off by hinged doors, probably triggered by pressure on the nose leg. The engines then 'breathe' through the top of the wing normally closed by doors. This eliminates ingestion of slush and other material.

Structurally, the vertical tails are mounted on the outer sides of the 'rear fuselage', which is actually the engine bay below wing level. No longer does the tail have to be detachable; the engines can be withdrawn to the rear. The main gears retract forwards with the wheels turning 90° to lie inside the wing root. The nose gear retracts backwards between the inlet ducts.

The wings have leading-edge flaps, plain flaps and outboard ailerons, only about 25° of flap being used for landing. Computers schedule the wing camber for maximum manoeuvrability, with the primary roll control at high speeds being the slab tailerons. The rudders are quite small. Each wing is attached to a blended inboard portion which extends forwards in an apex to provide a flat undersurface above the inlets. Most of the apex leading edge is occupied by RWRs, ESM antennas and other avionics. In the nose is the pulse-doppler radar. There are the usual comprehensive fits of IFF, ILS and communications, as well as a large IR sensor under a

Origin: Soviet Union.
Engines: Two Tumanskii R-33D each rated at 11,243lb (5,100kg) dry and 18,300lb (8,300kg) with max augmentation.
Dimensions: Span 37ft 9in (11.5m); length (inc probe) 56ft 5¼ in (17.2m); height 14ft 5in (4.4m); wing area 379ft² (35.2m²).
Weights: Empty 18,025lb (8,175kg); loaded (fighter mission) 36,375lb (16,500kg) max about 39,680lb (18,000kg).
Performance: (Estimated) Max speed (hi altitude) 1,525mph (2,455km/h, Mach 2.3), (sea level) 910mph (1,470km/h, Mach 1.2); max climb 50,000ft (15,240m)/min; combat radius (hi) 715 miles (1,150km).
Armament: One 30mm gun in left wing root; three pylons under each wing for six AA-10 medium-range radar-guided AAMs or six close-range AA-11 AAMs, or for wide range of attack stores.
History: First flight not later than April 1979; service entry October 1983.

Below: Five of the six MiG-29s from Kubinka airbase which on 1 July 1986 made the type's first public appearance, in Finland. Its second public showing was to be the 1988 Farnborough airshow in England.

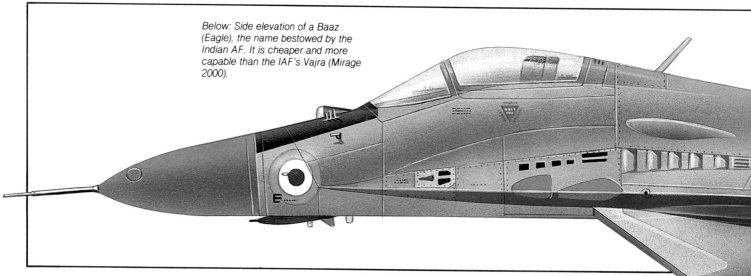

Below: Side elevation of a Baaz (Eagle), the name bestowed by the Indian AF. It is cheaper and more capable than the IAF's Vajra (Mirage 2000).

transparent dome offset to the right in front of the windshield.

A notable feature of this shape of aircraft (and thus of the Su-27 also) is the height of the fuselage, which means that ladders and trestles are needed for access to many LRUs (line replaceable units). The payoff is the superb engine installation, which plays a big part in making this one of the best air-combat fighters. But Soviet designers impede the pilot's view with devices inside and outside the cockpit.

By spring 1988 about 450 MiG-29s were probably in combat units. India has 40, and 2 of the dual trainer version which has only a small ranging radar, and expects Hindustan Aeronautics to build it under licence. Other early customers include Iraq, Syria and (it is reported) Zimbabwe.

Above: The first production MiG-29s had ventral tail fins, but these were omitted from all later types such as this example seen with twin AA-10

Alamo-A and quadruple AA-8 Aphid missiles. The latter missiles are being replaced by the new AA-11, called Archer by NATO.

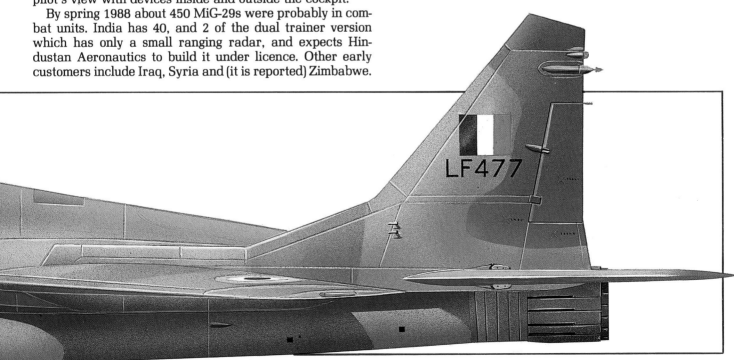

MiG-31 (Foxhound)

Though based closely on the MiG-25, the MiG-31 is a completely new aircraft. Structurally the airframe has been restressed for manoeuvrability at all altitudes. A unique feature is that the twin-wheel main landing gears are steerable. The MiG-31 can outrun almost anything else in the sky, and has a complete capability against multiple targets at all heights, including ground-hugging lo attack.

Among the major differences compared with the MiG-25 are the addition of a second crew member, the elimination of the wing-tip anti-flutter bodies and the ability to carry eight missiles. The AAMs are smaller than the AA-6 but have a similar punch and require no inflight guidance. MiG-31s have demonstrated great radar range and TWS capability while intercepting RPV targets including simulated cruise missiles at Vladimirovka, a test range on the Caspian. Another report states that radar-guided missiles fired from high-flying MiG-31s have intercepted targets flying at about 200ft (90m).

There are four wing pylons, and four on the flanks of the fuselage. Even the AA-9 is still a substantial missile, considerably bigger than Sparrow, and eight would impose a serious drag penalty. Four regiments of MiG-31s (about 150

aircraft) were already operational with Voyska PVO forces by late 1986, with output from a factory at Gorkii building up all the time.

In 1986 it was announced by the US Department of Defense that there is also a reconnaissance version, which one may assume to be the MiG-31R. Roughly one-quarter of the output is of this version. Both variants have an internal active jammer and countermeasures dispenser, while the interceptor has an IR sensor.

There may also be an ECM or other electronic-warfare version, as in the case of the MiG-25, but this is speculation.

Above: One of the latest photos of a MiG-31 interceptor, taken by a pilot of the Royal Norwegian AF. It carried four giant AA-9 AAMs.

Origin: Soviet Union.
Engines: Two Tumanskii R-31F each rated at 30,865lb (14,000kg).
Dimensions: (Estimated) Span 45ft 10½in (14m); length 70ft 6½in (21.5m); height 18ft 6in (5.63m); wing area 602ft² (56m²).
Weights: (Estimated) Empty 48,115lb (21,825kg); max 90,725lb (41,050kg).
Performance: (Estimated) Max speed (hi, 8 AAM) 1,586mph (2,553km/h, Mach 2.4), (sea level) 900mph (1,450km/h, Mach 1.18); service ceiling 75,500ft (23,000m); combat radius (hi, intercept) 1,305 miles (2,100km).
Armament: Eight AA-9 AAM, or four AA-9 and four R-23R or R60s.
History: First flight probably about 1977; service delivery 1981.

Below: Underside plan view of a MiG-31 showing wing-mounted AA-6 missiles. In fact the body-mounted AA-9 is much more common, though the older AA-6 missile is believed to be an alternative. So far as is known, this interceptor is not fitted with an internal gun.

Below: Side elevation of a MiG-31 showing underwing AA-6 Acrid missiles and drop tanks. In mid-1988 armament options were unknown.

Northrop F-5

Origin: United States.
Engines: Two General Electric J85 (A,B) 4,080lb (1,850kg) J85-13 or -13A, (E,F) 5,000lb (2,270kg) -21A.
Dimensions: Span (A,B over tip tanks) 25ft 10in (7.87m), (E,F over AAMs) 27ft 11in (8.53m); length (A) 47ft 2in (14.38m), (E) 48ft 2in (14.68m), (F) 51ft 7in (15.72m); height (E) 13ft 7in (4.06m); wing area (A,B) 170ft² (15.79m²), (E,F) 186ft² (17.3m²).
Weights: Empty (A) 8,085lb (3,667kg), (E) 9,683lb (4,392kg); max loaded (A) 20,576lb (9,333kg), (E) 24,722lb (11,214kg).
Performance: Max speed at 36,000ft (11,000m) (A) 925mph (1,489km/h, Mach 1.4), (E) 1,077mph (1,734km/h, Mach 1.63), initial climb (A,B) 28,700ft (8,750m)/min, (E) 34,500ft (10,516m)/min; service ceiling (all) about 51,000ft (15,540m); combat radius with max weapon load (A, hi-lo-hi) 215 miles (346km), (E, lo-lo-lo) 138 miles (222km).
Armament: (A,B) Military load 6,200lb (2,812kg) including two 20mm M-39 guns each with 280 rounds, and variety of underwing stores, plus AIM-9 AAMs for air combat; (E,F) wide range of ordnance to total of 7,000lb (3,175kg) not including two (F-5F, one) M-39A2 guns each with 280 rounds and two AIM-9 missiles on tip rails.
History: First flight (N-156C) 30 July 1959, (production F-5A) October 1963, (F-5E) 11 August 1972.

Cheap, simple, delightful to handle and supersonic, the small twin-jets from Northrop have found a ready market all over the world. The F-5A Freedom Fighter and F-5B tandem dual two-seater were followed by the F-5E Tiger II. This has a wider fuselage increasing internal fuel to 563.7gal (2,563l), leading-edge root extensions, uprated engines, an extensible nose leg, manoeuvre flaps, a gyro sight, an arrester hook and an Emerson radar with a fair capability against air or ship targets at ranges to 23 miles (37km).

Individual customers have asked for extras, Saudi Arabian aircraft having a more comprehensive avionics fit including a Litton INS, comprehensive RWR and chaff/flare dispensers and Maverick ASMs. Switzerland specified anti-skid brakes and a different ECM fit. Improvements that became standard during production included auto manoeuvre flaps on both leading and trailing edges, a flattened 'shark nose' and larger leading-edge extensions.

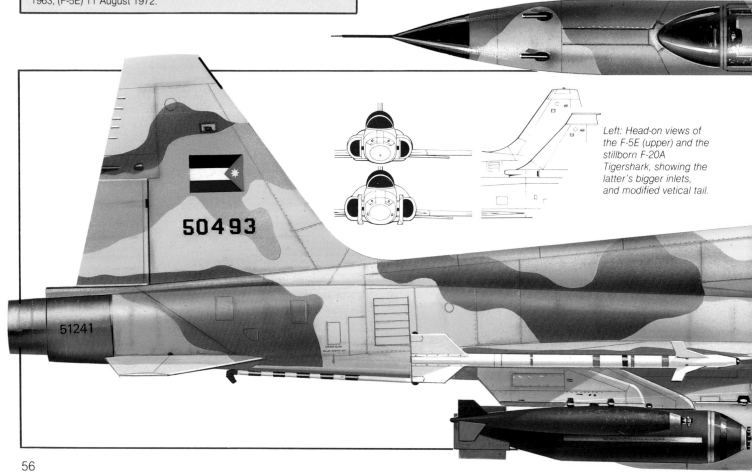

Left: Head-on views of the F-5E (upper) and the stillborn F-20A Tigershark, showing the latter's bigger inlets, and modified vetical tail.

50493

51241

The F-5F two-seater retains one gun and external weapons. The RF-5E Tigereye replaces the radar by a new, longer nose with a different profile in which can be installed a forward oblique KS-87D1 frame camera and any of a growing series of pallets on which are mounted selected sensors.

Product was completed in early 1987. Together with licensees, the total of all versions was 2,610.

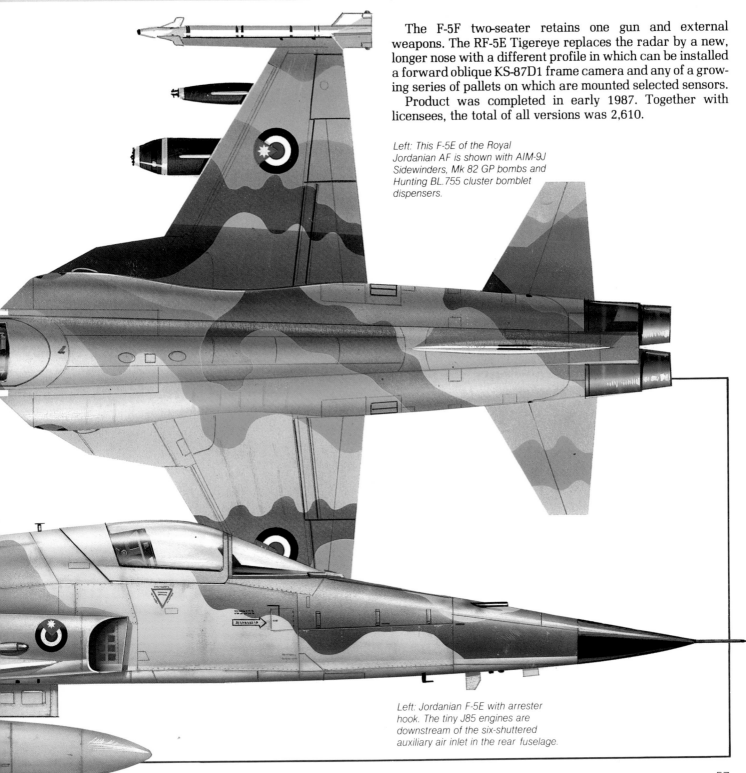

Left: This F-5E of the Royal Jordanian AF is shown with AIM-9J Sidewinders, Mk 82 GP bombs and Hunting BL.755 cluster bomblet dispensers.

Left: Jordanian F-5E with arrester hook. The tiny J85 engines are downstream of the six-shuttered auxiliary air inlet in the rear fuselage.

Panavia Tornado ADV

Though it was a British development, the ADV (air-defence variant) of Tornado is produced by the same tri-national airframe and engine groupings as the IDS series. It is the most efficient long-range interceptor in the world.

Designated Tornado F.3 by the RAF, it has about 80 per cent commonality with the IDS aircraft. The forward fuselage features new cockpits, with later displays, different symbology, greater processing and storage capacity and a wet-film HDD recorder; AI.24 Foxhunter FMICW radar, with multimode lookup/lookdown TWS and missile guidance capability; deletion of one gun; a permanent FR probe fully retractable on the left side; a ram-air turbine giving full hydraulic system power at high altitudes with main engines inoperative, down to below 230mph (370km/h); and the addition of new IFF, ECM-resistant data link (with an AWACS, for example), and a second INS.

Origin: European consortium.
Engines: Two Turbo-Union RB199 Mk 104, each rated at 18,100lb (8,212kg).
Dimensions: Span (25°) 45ft 7¼in (13.9m), (67°) 28ft 2½in (8.6m); length 59ft 4in (18.08m); height 18ft 8½in (5.7m); wing area not known.
Weights: Empty (equipped) 31,970lb (14,500kg); take-off (clean, max internal fuel) 47,500lb (21,546kg); max 61,700lb (27,986kg).
Performance: Max speed (clean, hi) about 1,500mph (2,414km/h, Mach 2.27); intercept radius (subsonic mission) over 1,151 miles (1,853km).
Armament: One 27mm Mauser cannon, four Sky Flash (later AMRAAM) and two or four AIM-9L Sidewinder AAMs (later ASRAAM).
History: First flight 27 October 1979; service delivery late 1984.

Other airframe changes include the forward extension of the fixed wing gloves, giving a major change in lift and agility, 200gal (909l) extra fuel in the extended fuselage, and belly recesses for four Sky Flash missiles, with twin-ram, ejection giving clean launch at maximum negative g. The engines have various upratings which at high speeds and altitudes become significant, with digital control.

By mid-1984 British Aerospace had delivered the first two F.2 production aircraft. The latter were ATs (dual pilot ADV trainers). The first production batch of 15 was complete by this time, with Mk 103 engines. The second and third batches, numbering 52 and 92 aircraft and designated F.3, have the Mk 104 from the outset, as well as automatic schedule of wing-sweep and manoeuvre-devices. Updates

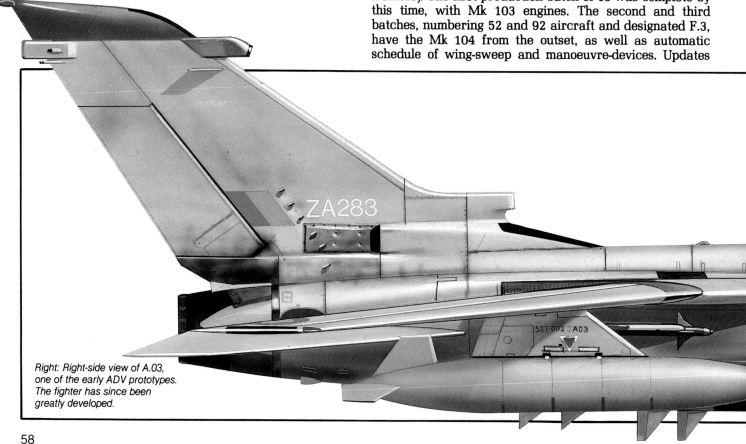

Right: Right-side view of A.03, one of the early ADV prototypes. The fighter has since been greatly developed.

planned for the future include still more powerful engines, even larger (495gal/2,250l) drop tanks, new missiles and further improvements to the avionics.

From early 1986 the Tornado F.3 began protecting the UK Air Defence Region though the radar needed a "get well" programme. The first export order was eight for the Sultan of Oman's Air Force; later the same year (1985) a contract for 24 was signed by Saudi Arabia. With 165 for the RAF, this makes a total of 197, to which will probably be added 40 for Italy.

Left: One of the early F.3 deliveries was ZE288, to 29 Sqn. Their 'triple X' insignia is on the engine inlet. (Photo by Sq/Ldr Tony Paxton, RAF.)

Below: Looking down on an F.2. The F.3 differs mainly in having jetpipes 14in (356mm) longer, giving greater power at supersonic speeds.

Saab 35 Draken

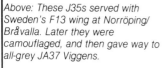

Above: These J35s served with Sweden's F13 wing at Norröping/Bråvalla. Later they were camouflaged, and then gave way to all-grey JA37 Viggens.

Amazingly bold in its conception in 1949-50, the Saab 35 Draken (Dragon) matured as a supremely good and cost-effective supersonic interceptor with excellent manoeuvrability at all heights, which for all intents and purposes does the same job as the British Lightning on just half the number of the same type of engine. Indeed the final version — the F-35 as bought by Denmark — does a great deal more, with the ability to put down nine 1,000lb (454kg) bombs with fair accuracy.

The main version still serving with the Swedish Flygvapen is the J35F (popularly Filip, and succeeding David, the J35D). The J35F was the most expensive of the six Swedish models, but also built in the largest numbers, the new equipment including an outstanding pulse-doppler radar. Hughes-derived fire control system and armed with a gun and both IR and radar-guided AAMs. Saab went on to build 606 Drakens in all, the final batches being for Finland and Denmark.

Origin: Sweden.
Engine: One Svenska Flygmotor RM6 (licence-built Rolls-Royce Avon with SFA afterburner): (D, E, F and export) 17,110lb (7,761kg) RM6C.
Dimensions: Span 30ft 10in (9.4m); length 50ft 4in (15.4m) (S35E, 52ft, 15.8m); height 12ft 9in (3.9m); wing area 529.6ft² (49.2m²).
Weights: Empty (D) 16,017lb; (F) 18,180lb (8,250kg); maximum loaded (D) 22,663lb (10,280kg); (F) 27,050lb (12,270kg); (F-35) 35,275lb (16,000kg).
Performance: Max speed (D onwards, clean) 1,320mph (2,125km/h, Mach 2.0), (with two drop tanks and two 1,000lb bombs) 924mph (1,487km/h, Mach 1.4); initial climb (D onwards, clean) 34,450ft (10,500m)/min; service ceiling (D onwards, clean) about 65,000ft (20,000m); range (internal fuel plus external weapons, typical) 800 miles (1,300km), (maximum fuel) 2,020 miles (3,250km).
Armament: (F) one 30mm Aden plus two RB27 Falcon (radar) and two RB28 Falcon (infra-red) missiles, plus two or four RB24; (F-35) two 30mm Aden plus nine stores pylons each rated at 1,000lb (454kg) all usable simultaneously, plus four RB24.
History: First flight 25 October 1955; (production J35A) 15 February 1948; final delivery (35XS) 1975, (Danish TF-35) 1976.

Left: One of the F-35 Draken fighter/ bombers serving with 725 Sqn of the Royal Danish AF, and recently upgraded for continued service into the 1990s.

Below: Side elevation of a 'Filip' serving with Sweden's F10 wing at Anmgelholm/Barkakra. It is carrying Swedish Sidewinder and Falcon AAMs.

Finland initially purchased 12 of the latest type, designated J35s, which were locally assembled by the Valmet company at Tampere and equip No 11 Sqn at Rovaniemi. Subsequently, in 1984, a further 23 ex Swedish aircraft were purchased, of the J35C and J35F versions, which serve with 21 Sqn at Tampere. Finland also has six J35BS trainers.

Denmark found the Swedish machine not only extremely low-priced but also so good it is remaining in front-line use alongside the F-16 until at least 1987-88, while the F-100s and F-104s have been replaced.

Three versions are in use, each having a counterpart in the Flygvapen with minor changes. The basic fighter-bomber is the F-35, serving with 725 Sqn in the Karup wing and backed by two-seat dual TF-35 conversion trainers which have limited weapons capability. The RF-35, whose Swedish partner is the S35E, is a reconnaissance fighter which normally carries the Red Baron night recon multisensor pod.

In 1987-88 Saab devoted 20,000 man-hours per aircraft to refurbishing 24 J35Ds for the Austrian air force. Redesignated as Saab 35OEs, they are expected to remain operational until the end of the century. Meanwhile, Saab and FFV Aerotech are refurbishing 50 J35Fs to the new J35J standard, to re-equip the three squadrons of F10 wing from 1989 until replacement by the Gripen in about 1998. Avionics, weapons and cockpit are all considerably upgraded.

All Draken versions have short field-length capability and are cleared for off-airfield operation, and in Sweden it is routine to operate from country highways and even farm roads. Drakens in service have been structurally audited to go on into the late 1980s, and avionics improvements have been incorporated, including HUD sights. Danish Fs and RFs even have INS, laser ranger and many subsystems similar to those equipping F-16s.

Saab JA37 Viggen

The final version of the Viggen, the JA37 fighter is a more extensive redesign than previous variants. Its performance is optimized for interception at a distance, using radar-guided medium-range Sky Flash AAMs, and for close combat at all altitudes.

The engine has a different match of fans and compressors, and gives higher thrust. The airframe has underwing fairings for four elevon power units on each wing instead of three, and the vertical tail (which folds flat for entry into underground hangars) is the same type as on the SK37 trainer.

Avionics stand comparison with those of any other fighter in service. The main radar is a UAP-1023 pulse-doppler set operating in I/J-band and giving look-down performance against low-flying small targets in adverse environments and in the presence of intense ECM (the same can, of course, be said of the Sky Flash missile). Other equipment includes an advanced HUD, main digital computer, digital air-data computer, advanced ILS, and comprehensive EW systems

Origin: Sweden.
Engine: One Volvo Flygmotor RM8B rated at 16,203lb (7,350kg) dry and 28,108lb (12,750kg) max.
Dimensions: Span 34ft 9⅓in (10.6m); length 53ft 9¾in (16.4m); height 19ft 4⅓in (5.9m); wing area 495.1ft² (46m²), foreplanes 66.74ft² (6.2m²).
Weights: Empty, not published; loaded (clean) about 33,070lb (15,000kg); 'with normal armament' about 37,478lb (17,000kg).
Performance: Max speed with AAMs (hi altitude) over 1,320mph (2,135km/h, Mach 2), (sea level) 910mph (1,470km/h Mach 1.2); tactical radius (external armament, hi-lo-hi) over 620 miles (1,000km), (lo-lo-lo) over 311 miles (500km).
Armament: One 30mm Oerlikon KCA cannon with 150 rounds; three body pylons and four underwing, for two RB71 (BAe Sky Flash) and four RB24 (AIM-9 Sidewinder) AAMs; plus rocket capability.
History: First flight (modified AJ development aircraft) 1974, (production JA) 4 November 1977; squadron delivery 1979.

(which make those of many NATO aircraft look pathetic). The single gun, under the fuselage, is very powerful.

The JA37 normally flies with a large drop tank, and it can carry surface-attack weapons. Air-superiority grey is being retroactively applied to aircraft in service. Deliveries of 149 JA37s were made to Wings F4, F13, F16, F17 and F21 in 1979-88.

Left: Head-on views of the JA37 fighter and (upper) the AJ37 attack aircraft, showing how the vertical tail can be folded to permit entry into low 'hides'.

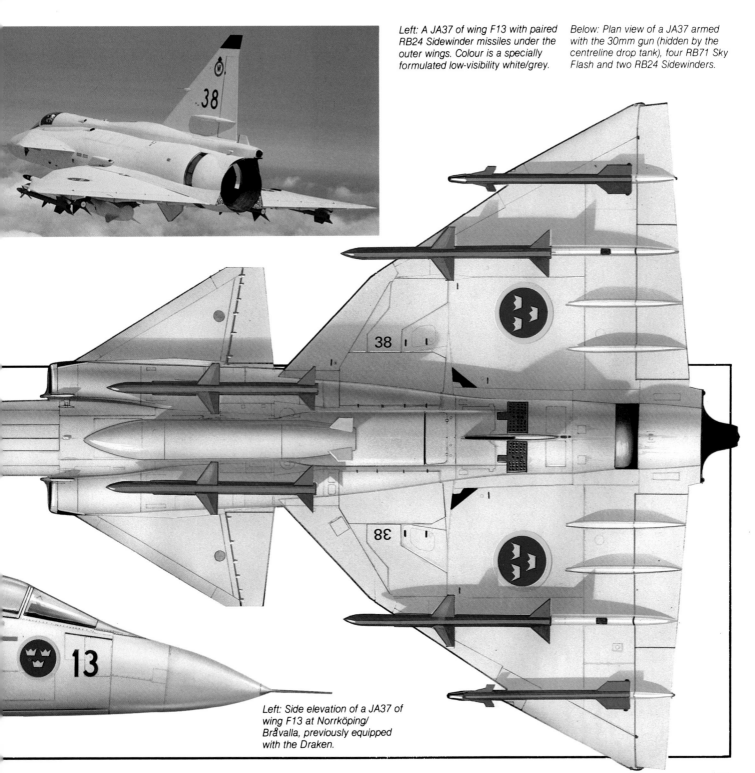

Left: A JA37 of wing F13 with paired RB24 Sidewinder missiles under the outer wings. Colour is a specially formulated low-visibility white/grey.

Below: Plan view of a JA37 armed with the 30mm gun (hidden by the centreline drop tank), four RB71 Sky Flash and two RB24 Sidewinders.

Left: Side elevation of a JA37 of wing F13 at Norrköping/ Bråvalla, previously equipped with the Draken.

Saab JAS39 Gripen

The JAS 39 designation signifies Jakt (fighter), Attack, Span-ing (reconnaissance). It is the smallest of all current fighters, but it will have all-round capability exceeding even that of the Viggen.

About 30 per cent of the airframe is high-strength com-posites. British Aerospace is chief sub-contractor for the wing, which is largely of carbon-fibre and is provided with powered leading and trailing surfaces for maximum combat agility.

In conjunction with the fully powered, foreplanes this wing should give the Gripen (Griffon) a combat agility equalling that of any rival. Having control surfaces both ahead of and behind the centre of gravity is expected to lead to the ability to change attitude or trajectory independently. The single-wheel landing gears, designed for no-flare landings, with a braked nosewheel, confer the ability to operate in the worst weather, from rough airstrips, highways and dirt roads.

Origin: Sweden.
Engine: One Volvo Flygmotor RM12 rated at 18,100lb (8,210kg).
Dimensions: (Approximate) Span 26ft 3in (8m); length 46ft 3in (14.1m); height 15ft 5in (4.7m).
Performance: Max speed (hi) about 1,320mph (2,135km/h, Mach 2), (sea level) supersonic; required field length, 2,625ft (800m).
Armament: One 27mm Mauser BK27 gun; four wing pylons for RB71 Sky Flash AAMs, RBS15F anti-ship missiles or other attack loads; wing-tip rails for RB24 Sidewinder AAMs.
History: First flight June 1988.

The cockpit will have a Martin-Baker S10LS seat, Hotas controls, diffractive-optics HUD and three electronic displays, reprogrammable by the pilot. Other features include fly-by-wire controls (tested in a Viggen), rear-fuselage airbrakes, plain lateral inlets, multimode radar and optional pod-mounted FLIR and laser ranger (which together handle the reconnaissance mission, apart from pod-mounted optical cameras), and comprehensive internal and external EW systems.

The RM12, derived from the F404, has improved resistance to bird ingestion. A triply redundant FBW system, with analog back-up, controls the canards, leading and trailing wing flaps and rudder. About 30 computers are connected to a flexible data bus. Microcomputers handle such systems as flight control, air data, fuel, inertial navigation, environmental control and hydraulics. The auxiliary and emergency power system, comprises a gearbox-mounted turbine, hydraulic pump and AC generator. In the emergency modes the turbine is driven either by engine bleed or APU air, or using stored, pressurized oxygen and methanol fuel. The APU is a gas turbine.

By year 2000 it is hoped that a force of 140 Gripens can be deployed, including about 25 tandem dual-pilot versions, at an estimated cost of SKr 25 billion. The first of five prototypes was due to fly before this book appears, and service is scheduled for 1992–93.

Above left: Looking up at a JAS39 as it will appear in combat service, showing RBS15F anti-ship missiles, an ECM jammer pod and a chaff dispenser.

Above: The Gripen prototype was rolled out in the spring of 1987, but was then subjected to prolonged testing in readiness for a first flight in mid-1988.

Below: Side elevation of a JAS39 as it might appear when in service with wing F17 at Ronneby in the 1990s. Sweden could sell large numbers.

Shenyang J-6 (Farmer)

The MiG-19 has wings swept at 53° yet fitted with outboard ailerons as well as high-lift flaps. The fuselage widens towards the rear to accommodate two slim engines and the horizontal tail is of the slab type. The levered-suspension landing gears have a wide track, and a large door-type airbrake is hinged under the belly.

China bought a licence in 1958, calling the basic MiG-19S fighter the J-6. This entered Chinese service in mid-1962. Subsequently several thousand J-6 variants have been built, almost all after 1966. Later models are the J-6A, with limited all-weather capability; the J-6B, with guns replaced by four K-5M AAMs; the J-6C day fighter, with the braking parachute relocated beneath the rudder; the J-6Xin ('J-6 new'), with radar in a slim radome; the JJ-6 dual trainer, with a flat-topped canopy hinged to the right; and the JZ-6 fighter-reconnaissance aircraft, with the nose gun replaced by two cameras.

Many still serve with the PLA (People's Liberation Army) Air Force and Navy, and with several other air forces. Export versions are designated F-6 (the trainer being the FT-6), and among many local modifications is an underbelly fuel tank in the Pakistan Air Force. Several users have their F-6s equipped to fire Sidewinder AAMs, and various Western manufacturers of avionics and other mission equipment are involved in update programmes, particularly with the Egyptian Air Force.

Below: With 140 supplied, Pakistan was the biggest export customer, though most were early versions with the drag chute under the fuselage.

Origin: Soviet Union and China.
Engines: Two Shenyang WP-6 each with max rating of 7,165lb (3,250kg).
Dimensions: Span 30ft 2⅓in (9.2m); length 48ft 10½in (14.9m), (JJ) 44ft 1in (13.4m); height 12ft 8¾in (3.88m); wing area 269.1ft² (25m²).
Weights: (Basic J-6) Empty 12,700lb (5,760kg); loaded (two tanks and two Sidewinders) 19,764lb (8,965kg), (max loaded) 22,046lb (10,000kg).
Performance: (J-6) Max speed (clean, hi) 955mph (1,540km/h, Mach 1.45), (clean, lo) 832mph (1,340km/h); initial climb over 30,000ft (9,144m)/ min; service ceiling 58,725ft (17,900m); combat radius (hi, two tanks) 426 miles (685km).
Armament: (J-6) Three Type 30-1 guns (30mm calibre), each with 80 rounds; four wing pylons, for Sidewinder or AA-2 'Atoll' AAMs or 500lb (227kg) bombs, rockets or tanks of 251gal (1,140l) size.
History: First flight (Soviet) 18 September 1953, (J-6) December 1961.

Below: All Pakistan AF J-6s carried bold unit markings, even when the unit was a training school. They have been retrofitted with the latest Martin-Baker Mk 10 ejection seats.

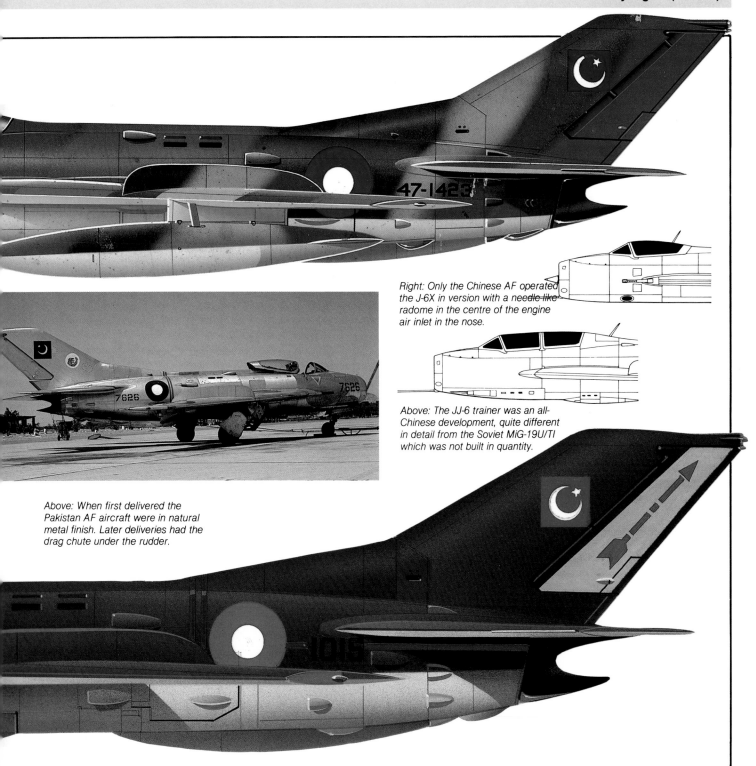

47-1423

Right: Only the Chinese AF operated the J-6X in version with a needle like radome in the centre of the engine air inlet in the nose.

Above: The JJ-6 trainer was an all-Chinese development, quite different in detail from the Soviet MiG-19U/TI which was not built in quantity.

7626

Above: When first delivered the Pakistan AF aircraft were in natural metal finish. Later deliveries had the drag chute under the rudder.

Shenyang J-8 (Finback)

Having acquired experience with the J-7 (based upon the MiG-21F) the Chinese decided in the mid-1960s to follow the Soviet MiG design bureau and produce a 'stretched' version with twin engines. The Soviet MiG Ye-152A remained a prototype, but the Chinese J-8 I was put into limited production, an estimated 50 having been put into service.

After considerable further thought it was decided to develop the J-8 II. This promised to rectify two major shortcomings. The new lateral inlets and ducts leave the nose free for radar and serve engines of greater thrust, based on the Tumanskii R-13-300. Likewise, the Type 23-3 gun is a Chinese version of the Soviet GSh-23L, mounted aft of the nose landing gear. The folding ventral fin closely resembles that of the MiG-23.

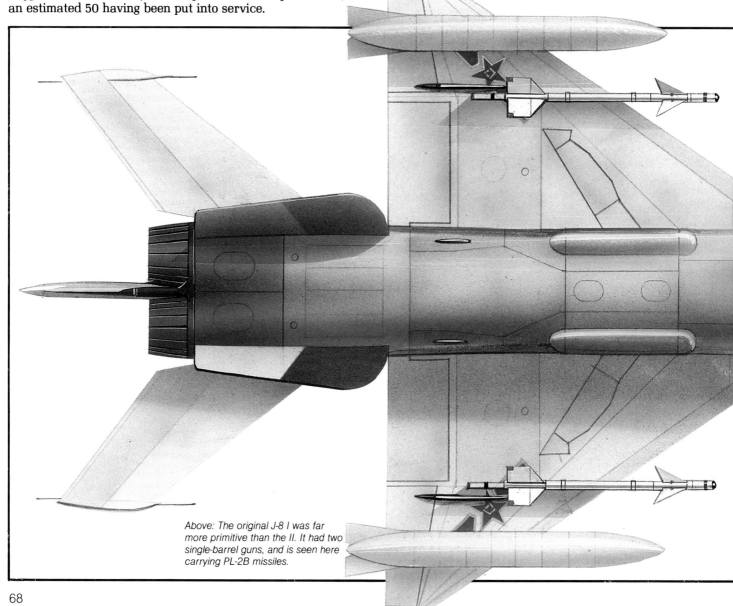

Above: The original J-8 I was far more primitive than the II. It had two single-barrel guns, and is seen here carrying PL-2B missiles.

Origin: China.
Engines: Two Wopen 13A-II each rated at 14,815lb (6,720kg).
Dimensions: Span 30ft 8in (9.34m); length (inc nose probe) 70ft 10in (21.59m); height 17ft 9in (5.41m); wing area 454.2ft² (42.2m²).
Weights: Empty 21,649lb (9,820kg); normal loaded (fighter mission) 31,526lb (14,300kg); max 39,242lb (17,800kg).
Performance: Max speed (clean, hi altitude) 1,450mph (2,335km/h, Mach 2.2), (lo) 808mph (1,300km/h, Mach 1.06); initial climb 39,370ft (12,000m)/min; service ceiling 65,600ft (20,000m); combat radius 497 miles (800km); max range 1,367 miles (2,200km).
Armament: One Type 23-3 gun with 200 rounds; seven pylons for stores up to unit weight of 1,102lb (500kg).
History: First flight (J-8) believed 1969, (J-8 II) May 1984.

Lacking indigenous equipment, the Chinese industry concluded a deal with the US Department of Defense for 50 shipsets, plus five spare kits, each comprising a radar, inertial navigation system, avionics data bus, air data system and a HUD. These would be the main items for the first batch to be delivered in 1991–95. In service the Dash-IIs will each carry the gun, a centreline tank, two PL-2B missiles (derived from the Sidewinder) and two PL-7 missiles (resembling the Matra Magic but with semi-active radar guidance).

No exports are permitted with the US avionics fitted, but when an exportable version appears (with Chinese or alternative Western avionics) it will be designated F-8 II.

Left: Side elevation of one of the early Dash-I aircraft, development of which began in the mid-1960s. The II dates from about 1979.

Right: Takeoff by the prototype J-8 II. In early 1989 two pre-production aircraft are to be sent to Grumman to speed the update package.

Sukhoi Su-15, 21 ('Flagon')

Origin: Soviet Union.
Engines: Two Tumanskii R-13F2-300s, each rated at 15,875lb (7,200kg).
Dimensions: Span 34ft 6in (10.53m); length (inc probe) 68ft (20.5m); height 16ft 7in (5.05m); wing area 385ft² (35.7m²).
Weights: Empty about 22,490lb (10,200kg); loaded (clean) about 35,275lb (16,000kg), (max with external tanks) 39,990lb (18,140kg).
Performance: Max speed (clean, 36,000ft/11,000m), about 1,650mph (2,655km/h, Mach 2.5); (with AAMs) about 1,380mph (2,230km/h, Mach 2.1); initial climb 45,000ft (13,700m)/min; service ceiling 65,600ft (20,000m); combat radius (hi) about 450 miles (725km).
Armament: Four pylons for two medium-range AAMs (AA-3 'Anab' or R-23R/AA-7 'Apex', each in both IR and radar versions) and two or four close-range AAMs (R-60/AA-8 'Aphid') on the inners; two body pylons for tanks or GSh-23L gun pods, each with 200 rounds.
History: First flight late 1965; service delivery about 1969.

Via the single-engined Su-9 and -11, the Su-15 was developed to provide twin-engine safety and greater thrust, to make room for more internal fuel, and leave the nose free for a large radar. Like all PVO machines, it was designed to operate from long paved runways, so it has a high wing loading. This goes well with the mission of stand-off interception, but eliminates dogfight performance and also results in high take-off/landing speeds. Anti-skid brakes with computer control are fitted, together with a cruciform brake chute.

Aircraft in current service have a wing of increased span, with a midspan kink and reduced sweep outboard, and are believed to be designated Su-21. They also have twin nosewheels, a later radar (called 'Twin Scan' by NATO) in a curved ogival radome, and uprated engines fed by improved inlet ducts. Missiles have been updated and gun pods added. The tandem trainer version has the NATO name 'Flagon-G' instead of a name beginning with 'M', suggesting that it has full combat capability.

About 750 have been in use for many years, but the numbers are falling rapidly. Their only major shortcoming is that the mission radius is not great enough to cover the whole of the Soviet Union's vast frontier.

Above: The first production versions were distinguished by this curious conical radome. Later models had an ogival shape giving lower drag.

It was an Su-21 from a PVO regiment in the Far East that on 1 September 1983 shot down Korean Air Lines Flight 007, inward bound to Seoul, killing the 269 on board. A USAF RC-135 had been near the area, but there can have been little confusion over the identity of the 747.

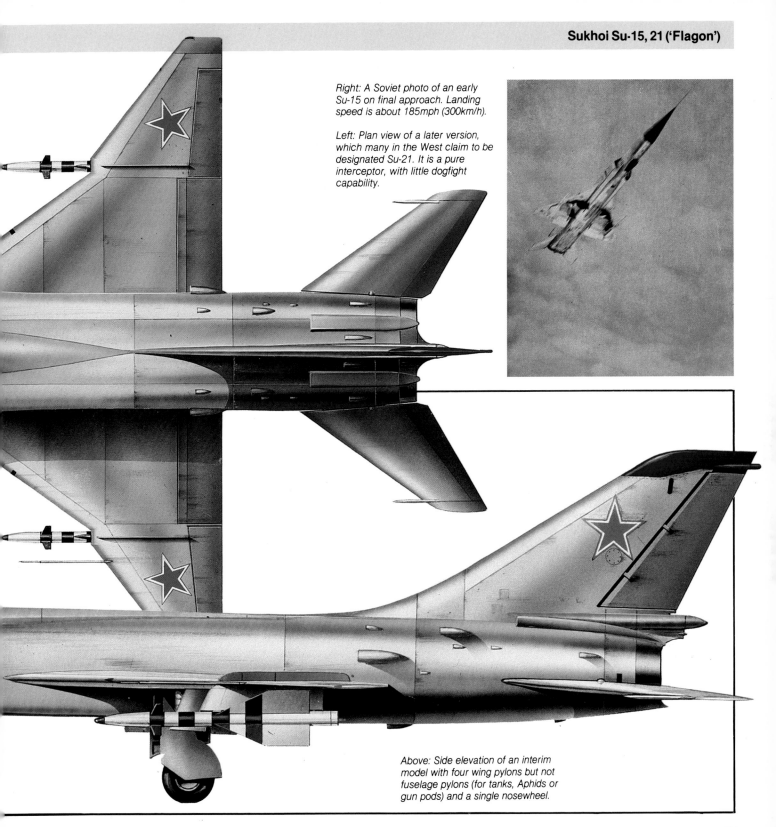

Right: A Soviet photo of an early Su-15 on final approach. Landing speed is about 185mph (300km/h).

Left: Plan view of a later version, which many in the West claim to be designated Su-21. It is a pure interceptor, with little dogfight capability.

Above: Side elevation of an interim model with four wing pylons but not fuselage pylons (for tanks, Aphids or gun pods) and a single nosewheel.

Sukhoi Su-27 (Flanker)

The biggest and most powerful Soviet fighter apart from the MiG-25/31, the Su-27 is based on the same aerodynamics as the MiG-29. Compared with the MiG-29, the Su-27 is almost twice as big (in area terms, i.e. a 1.4 linear scale), twice as heavy and twice as powerful.

Despite its size, accepted in order to achieve long mission radius with many weapons, giving great persistence in air combat, the Su-27 is generally considered to be able to outfly the MiG-29, which itself was specifically designed to beat the F-14, F-15, F-16 and F-18 in close combat (and is generally accepted as being capable of doing so).

The Su-27 has a completely new pulse-doppler multimode radar with the greatest possible performance against low-flying targets, and a track-while-scan capability out to a range of 150 miles (240km).

The Su-27 can carry 10 AAMs, including the short- and long-burn radar and the IR version of the big AA-10 Alamo. This is the first Soviet AAM which, in its radar-guided versions, has its own active seeker. Thus it can be fired against a distant hostile aircraft in the desired 'fire and forget' manner, the Su-27 then either engaging other targets or turning away: there is no need to keep flying towards the enemy in order to illuminate the target with the fighter's own radar. This capability will not arrive in Western squadrons until the AIM-120A (AMRAAM) becomes operational in, it is hoped, 1989. The Soviet weapon system was declared operational in late 1986. It includes an IR search/track sensor and magnifying optics.

There is probably a tandem two-seat Su-27, and a reconnaissance pod or pallet can doubtless be carried. This aircraft is in production at Komsomolsk, in the Far East. The Su-27 is seen as possible equipment for the large new aircraft carrier which was about to start sea trials as this book was written in 1988. By that time about 190 Su-27s were estimated to have been delivered.

Origin: Soviet Union.
Engines: Two Tumanskii R-32s of 29,955lb (13,600kg).
Dimensions: (Estimated) Span 48ft 3in (14.7m); length (exc probe) 70ft 10½in (21.6m); height 18ft (5.5m); wing area 690ft² (64m²).
Weights: (Estimated) Empty 33,000lb (15,000kg); internal fuel 14,330lb (6,500kg); loaded (air-to-air mission) 44,000lb (19,960kg); (max, surface attack) 77,200lb (35,000kg).
Performance: (Estimated) Max speed (hi, air-to-air mission) 1,350kt (DoD figure, converting to 1,555mph (2,500km/h, Mach 2.35); combat radius (air-to-air mission, four AA-10) 930 miles (1,500km).
Armament: Up to 10 AAMs of various types including six AA-10; one 30mm gun; in attack role, up to 13,225lb (6,000kg) of stores.
History: First flight probably about 1976; production initiation 1983.

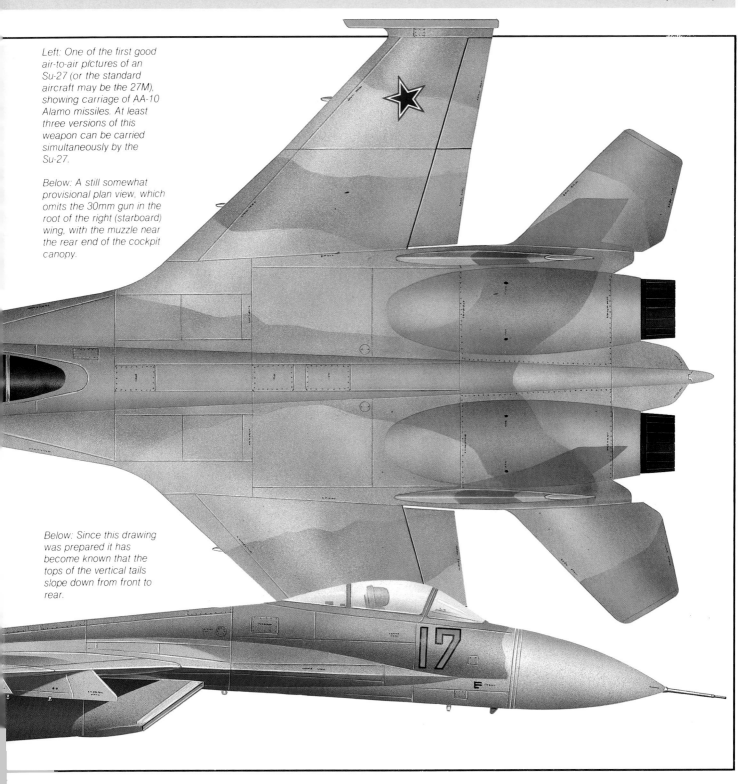

Left: One of the first good air-to-air pictures of an Su-27 (or the standard aircraft may be the 27M), showing carriage of AA-10 Alamo missiles. At least three versions of this weapon can be carried simultaneously by the Su-27.

Below: A still somewhat provisional plan view, which omits the 30mm gun in the root of the right (starboard) wing, with the muzzle near the rear end of the cockpit canopy.

Below: Since this drawing was prepared it has become known that the tops of the vertical tails slope down from front to rear.

Vought F-8E (FN) Crusader

Below: Apart from France the only other recent operator was the Philippines, which withdrew its 24 ex-US Navy F-8H fighters in late 1987.

The Vought team was picked from eight rivals in 1953 to build the US Navy's first supersonic carrier-based fighter. Despite having all the penalties of shipboard operation, the F-8 greatly outperformed the land-based F-100 of the same era, using an almost identical engine and despite having 1,165gal (5,300l) of internal fuel. One of its features was that the wing was mounted above the fuselage and pivoted so that its incidence could be varied. This enabled the aircraft to approach with the fuselage nose-down, giving the pilot an excellent forward view, and enabling short main landing gears to be used, retracting into the fuselage.

Most of the 1,259 aircraft built have been retired, the last (land-based) user being the Philippines, with 34 refurbished ex-US Navy F-8H fighters. In France, however, the Aéronavale not only still flies the specially developed F-8E(FN) but can see no obvious replacement until the Rafale M becomes available at the end of the century.

The F-8E(FN) was specially tailored to enable it to operate from the small carriers of the French navy, the *Clemenceau* and *Foch*. The wing was modified with two-stage leading-edge flaps and main flaps all with larger angles of travel, backed up by engine-bleed BLC (boundary-layer control) blowing to enable approach speed to be reduced. There are many other differences, including on-board avionics matched to the French R.530 and Magic missiles. The Aéronavale purchased 42 Crusaders. In 1969 it contracted with LTV (Vought) for new wing panels, with thicker skins, titanium wing-fold ribs and other changes, cleared for a further 4,000 flight hours.

Below left: Today the French Navy (Aéronavale) operates its Crusaders in dull grey overall, with reduced-visibility stencilling.

Above: Aircraft No 29 on final approach, a Magic AAM on its rack below the large blister over the retracted flight-refuelling probe.

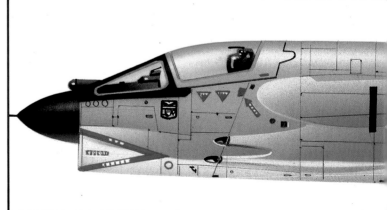

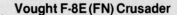

Origin: United States.
Engines: One Pratt & Whitney J57-P-20A turbojet, with a maximum rating of 18,000lb (8,165kg) thrust with afterburner.
Dimensions: Span 35ft 2in (10.72m); length 54ft 6in (16.61m); height 15ft 9in (4.8m); wing area 375ft² (34.84m²).
Weights: Empty 19,700lb (8,935kg); maximum loaded 34,000lb (15,420kg).
Performance: Max speed (hi, clean) 1,135mph (1,827km/h, Mach 1.7); initial climb about 21,000ft (6,400m)/min; combat radius (typical) 440 miles (708km).
Armament: Four 20mm Colt Mk 12 cannon, each with 84 or 144 rounds, plus Sidewinder or Matra Magic close-range AAMs on fuselage side pylons, plus two Matra R.530D or Super 530 medium-range AAMs on underwing pylons. Option of carrying bombs or rocket launchers or cluster dispensers not normally used.
History: First flight (XF8U-1) 25 March 1955; (production F-8A) November 1956, (F-8E/FN) 26 June 1964. Final delivery to French navy January 1965.

This proved a sound move, but it was not then appreciated how long the Crusaders would have to serve. The Rafale M is still rather uncertain, and in any case cannot replace the Crusaders until at least 1997. All calculations indicate that, on any reasonable flying rate, the Crusaders cannot last that long, but purchase of an interim type (the Hornet has been suggested) would be very costly and uneconomic.

Below: Side elevation of an F-8E(FN) in the original paint scheme, which was based on that of the US Navy. Radar is the Magnavox APQ-94.

Yakovlev Yak-38 (Forger)

This V/STOL shipboard aircraft is more versatile than originally thought, and carries greater loads. The version called 'Forger-B' differs in being a tandem two-seater thought to be used for pilot training but possibly serving in EW and other operational roles. This version lacks the radar and ordnance pylons.

Take-off and landing are often vertical, but rolling launches can be flown with precision guidance. The main pair of nozzles are vectored forwards up to 10° to balance the rearward thrust of the inclined lift jets behind the cockpit. Landings are also electronically guided: each approach from astern is at quite a low closing speed in level flight about 40ft (12m) above deck level, the final landing being vertical. Avionics include a ranging radar, radar altimeters, inertial and doppler navigation, and comprehensive IFF and electronic-warfare systems.

The aircraft's primary missions are believed to be the destruction of ocean patrol and ASW aircraft, anti-ship attack and reconnaissance. Up to 12 of these machines have been observed aboard each of the large VTOL carriers *Kiev*, *Minsk*, *Novorossisk* and *Baku*.

Above: One of the best photos available of Yak-38s (of the first production batch, without dorsal fences around the lift-engine air inlets).

Below: This side elevation again shows the initial sub-type without dorsal fences, but it shows AA-2 Atoll (K-13A) AAMs on wing pylons.

Origin: Soviet Union.
Engines: One vectored-thrust Lyulka AL-21 rated at 17,985lb (8,160kg), plus two Koliesov ZM lift jets each rated at 7,875lb (3,570kg).
Dimensions: (Estimated) Span 24ft (7.32m); length (A) 50ft 10¼in (15.5m), (B) 58ft (17.68m); height 14ft 4in (4.37m); wing area 199.14ft².
Weights: (Estimated) Empty (A) 16,500lb (7,485kg), (B) 18,500lb (8,390kg); max (both) 25,794lb (11,700kg).
Performance: (Estimated) Max speed (clean, hi) 627mph (1,009km/h, Mach 0.95), (clean, sea level) 647mph (1,041km/h, Mach 0.85); initial climb 14,750ft (4,500m)/min; service ceiling 39,370ft (12,000m); combat radius (max weapons, lo-lo-lo) 150 miles (240km).
Armament: All carried on four pylons, including GSh-23L gun pods, AA-8 'Aphid' (R-60) close-range AAMs, rocket launchers or bombs to total of 7,936lb (3,600kg), or AS-7 'Kerry' ASMs.
History: First flight probably 1971; service delivery about 1975.

Above: Pilots salute on receiving their orders aboard a ship of the Kiev class. Their Yak-38s are ready for boarding but have their wing pylons unloaded.

Left: Parked on the deck of Minsk are later Yak-38s with long fences along each side of the lift-engine inlets. Colour is dark grey/ blue.

Index

PRINTED IN BELGIUM BY

proost
INTERNATIONAL BOOK PRODUCTION